One Nation Under BLOG

One Nation Under BLOG

Forget the Facts . . . Believe What I Say!

David Wallace

BROWN BOOKS
PUBLISHING GROUP
Dallas, Texas

ONE NATION UNDER BLOG
FORGET THE FACTS . . .
BELIEVE WHAT I SAY!

Manufactured in the United States of America.

For information, please contact:
Brown Books Publishing Group
16200 North Dallas Parkway, Suite 170
Dallas, Texas 75248
www.brownbooks.com
972-381-0009

A New Era in Publishing™

Hardbound ISBN-13: 978-1-934812-09-9
Hardbound ISBN-10: 1-934812-09-9

Paperback ISBN-13: 978-1-934812-10-5
Paperback ISBN-10: 1-934812-10-2

LCCN: 2008928543

1 2 3 4 5 6 7 8 9 10

DEDICATION

To Kathy, my wife, and Whitney and Jacquelyn, my daughters, who have lived through the fun, excitement, and intrigue of the life and times of a public official. I chose to enter public life and all the wonder that it entails. You were the innocent bystanders who supported me through challenging times and celebrated with me in the victories.

TABLE OF CONTENTS

FORGET THE FACTS . . . BELIEVE WHAT I SAY!

I began this book out of personal concern and completed it with the hope that responsible free speech will prevail. In my enthusiasm for public service as mayor of a mid-size Texas town, I naively assumed that my good intentions would be evident and appreciated by others. As a businessman intent on saving companies on the brink of financial ruin, I hoped that my difficult decisions would be recognized as sound attempts to salvage failing enterprises. Along the way, I found that free speech, especially in the form of Web logs, like any other freedom, can be abused, misused, and manipulated.

What I discovered initially discouraged me about the future use of communication technology. Harsh negative blogs written about me without basis in fact and later proven to be untrue damaged my reputation, hindered my effectiveness temporarily, and briefly tempered my enthusiasm for public service. The potential for anyone with a grudge to write anything about colleagues, neighbors, and public figures became the focus of my personal concern, but it soon broadened into a general fear for our children, our personal privacy, and our national safety.

What I learned is that negative Web logs linger in the blogosphere, often unchallenged and uncorrected, long after their writers have moved on to other interests and possibly other targets. The anonymity of both the bloggers and those who post comments can mean that responsibility for personal expression lies only with the character and integrity of the writer. Under the cloak of invisibility, bloggers do not face the same regulations, laws, or even monitoring that printed and spoken comments do. In short, the blogosphere exhibits a "Wild West" atmosphere without law and order.

What I hope will result from this book is an intense discussion of how blogs and their many offshoots are affecting our sense of security, our guardianship of our children, and our inclination to become public in any way. The freedom of speech that we all treasure so highly carries with it the duty to use it responsibly. Blogs can be a marvelous conduit for the people's voice. They can also demonstrate the worst aspects of irresponsibility. When we take advantage of communication technological advances willfully to harm others, we tarnish our democratic freedom. When we write in disguise and anonymously, we abdicate our right to stand up and be acknowledged.

As my understanding of the blogosphere and its potential grew, I broadened the scope of this book. Originally I thought of it as exploring my personal concern, but soon I realized the enormous significance of blogs and their potential impact on every aspect of our lives. From our children's comments on MySpace to an employee's discussion of internal corporate issues to rumors and innuendos on a homeowner's association blog, my research expanded, and my focus shifted. The result is *One Nation Under Blog: Forget the Facts . . . Believe What I Say!*

Part I "Free Speech in Cyberspace" traces the birth and growth of blogs and establishes their potential danger. Part II "Blogging the Past" imagines how our history might have changed if blogging technology had been available and used to target presidents like George Washington, Thomas Jefferson, Abraham Lincoln, John Kennedy, and Lyndon Johnson. Part III "Blogging in the MySpace Era" traces the rapid expansion and use of blogs for influencing public opinion. Part IV "Call to Action in Cyberspace" expresses my hope that bloggers will support, and readers will demand, a code of conduct that characterizes responsible blogs.

We value our fundamental principles of freedom, democracy, and rules of law. A powerful tool for freedom of speech has been given to us. How we use it will define us as Americans and offer a model for our children and grandchildren to follow. How will we lead them?

| PART 1 |

FREE SPEECH IN CYBERSPACE

*"Congratulations, it's an anonymous blow
to the character and credibility of your opponent."*

CHAPTER 1

THE BIRTH OF BLOG
MONICA LEWINSKY AND THE DRUDGE REPORT

BLOGGER'S CODE: TELL THE TRUTH, THE WHOLE TRUTH, AND NOTHING BUT THE TRUTH.

In January 1998, the Drudge Report began coverage on the Lewinsky-Clinton scandal in an uncensored, freedom-of-speech format that changed the course of online media forever. A tip leaked that *Newsweek* planned to kill the story about the White House intern and her sexual relationship with President Bill Clinton. The immoral ruckus gave birth to a new form of news distribution. Information flowed into the newsrooms instead of flowing out to the public. Drudge had the scoop of the century, and blogs were born.

Blogs give every citizen the opportunity to raise a voice. Combining technology and a sense of entitlement to be heard, blogs symbolize the twenty-first century version of freedom of speech. When Andrew Jackson opened the doors of the White House to the masses, he foreshadowed the impact blogging is having on democracy.

Communications technology has always played a crucial role in American life and politics. Where would we be without *Common Sense*, the printed pamphlet by Thomas Paine? Would Benjamin Franklin have been as influential without his best-selling *Poor Richard's Almanac*? If not for Paul Revere's famous engraving illustrating the Boston Massacre, what would have been the reaction to British soldiers shooting Boston civilians who were taunting them?

As an inventor, Franklin recognized the power of new technology. In 1754, he created and published the first modern political cartoon,

"Join or Die," in advance of that year's Albany Congress. Courageous printers distributed pamphlets, posters, and papers spreading the ideas that fueled the American Revolution. Technology gave voice to those who supported, and opposed, the founding of this country.

Over a century later as printing technology advanced, political parties created mass materials. In 1896, the Republican Party alone distributed millions of pamphlets. In that same year, transportation advances allowed William McKinley to conduct 350 speeches from his own front porch as railroads brought over 750,000 people to him. Four years later, Theodore Roosevelt successfully used the railway "whistle stop" delivery system to take his message to the voters.

Whistle stop tours quickly became standard fare for politicians, who would speak to assembled voters from the back of the train's caboose. Voters could size-up a candidate in person and "take the measure of the man." How a politician spoke, looked, and presented himself was just as important as the words he spoke. The stage was set for the public to demand more interactive communication with political and national figures.

The founding fathers may have had in mind some limitation on the "great unwashed masses," but with the advances in technology came expanded distribution of information and ideas through newspapers, radio, and television. Closer contact with political and national figures spurred readers, listeners, and viewers to form opinions and to find ways to talk back.

In 1963, the news went live with the assassination of President John F. Kennedy and the first on-camera murder of Lee Harvey Oswald by Jack Ruby. Suddenly viewers could witness major events from a distance and judge for themselves. No longer were they dependent on what others had seen and heard, accounts condensed and filtered through reporters' perspectives.

In the 1970s and 1980s, the development of the Internet brought about the capability for personal communication across the world, and that ability quickly expanded to voicing opinions on every aspect of American life. Jacksonian Democracy had been worked out in the extreme. Huey Long's statement, "Every Man, a King," now applied to communication. As Martin Luther once said, "With a Bible in his hand, every man is a Pope."

In 1995, Monica Lewinsky accepted an intern position in the White House and set in motion a series of events that changed the way the public receives news and how the news "breaks." Both Clinton and Lewinsky had denied a sexual liaison after Lewinsky's friend, Linda Tripp, exposed their secret through audiotapes. The probe became a scandal of national proportion.

When *Newsweek* scrubbed a story by Michael Isikoff, the online Drudge Report stepped in and revealed intimate details of the investigation and those involved, information that may otherwise have been hidden from public knowledge. In 1994, Matt Drudge had created the Report as a subscriber-based e-mail dispatch. In traditional media, the Drudge Report had been labeled a gossip column, but the Clinton/Lewinsky scoop sparked further press stories about the affair, which led to a special prosecutor, and the supposed cover-up.

Posted on January 17, 1998, under the title, "*Newsweek* Kills Story on White House Intern," the "blockbuster" report announced that a former White House intern had a sexual relationship with the President of the United States. Details included that she frequently visited a small study near the Oval Office where she "claims to have indulged the President's sexual preferences." The posting continued that she had been shifted to a job in the Pentagon when news of their liaison "spread in the White House quarters." Love letters, frequent late night visits, and taped intimate conversations had been part of the planned *Newsweek* article.

When the Drudge Report broke the news of the squashing of Isikoff's story and the relationship, other media outlets including the *Times* scrambled for their versions. The final line of the posting inaugurated a new era of blogs: "The White House was busy checking the Drudge Report for details." Access to information could no longer be mediated only by political parties, journalists, and major media.

This episode in communication evolution led to a new way for the Internet to be used: reporting on the reporters and checking the accuracy of their political coverage. The Drudge Report launched the age of blogging, where the individual not only generates the news but also keeps watch on those who wish to control it. The Drudge Report is now syndicated and links to international and national mainstream news stories.

Also in 1998, MoveOn.org started as an online petition to tell Congress that they should censure President Bill Clinton and "move on" past impeachment proceedings. Expecting a few thousand responses, they received half a million, and the basis for an online grass-roots organization was formed.

In 1999, what the Drudge Report accomplished for the content of online reporting and MoveOn achieved in Internet response, Pyra Labs expanded with the creation of a software product called "Blogger." With revolutionary insight, Pyra Labs reduced the technological requirements of Web publishing to the barest essentials, opening up the world of publishing to anyone with a laptop and a modem. That same year blogs were estimated to be no more than fifty, but in five years, they exploded to an estimated 4.1 million.

By 2006, blogs had raked in some impressive statistics:

- Adult bloggers in the United States reached 12 million (Pew Internet & American Life Project).

- Of blogs created, 92.4 percent were by people under the age of thirty, half by teens between thirteen and nineteen years of age with ages twenty to twenty-nine making up about 39.6 percent (The Perseus Report).

- Blogs had reached only about 10 percent of the Internet population (Gawker).

- A blog was created every minute (Wired News).

- Every second 2.3 content updates were posted (Wired News).

- The life of a blog often is short; 60–80 percent of blogs are abandoned within a month, and few are regularly updated. Males are most likely to abandon blogs at 46.4 percent (Perseus, "The Blogging Iceberg").

- Millions of blogs have no more than two dozen readers and are created for viewing only by friends, family, fellow students, and coworkers (The Perseus Report).

What these figures may not capture is the rapidly legitimizing of blogs as tools for political candidates, business customer service, patient sharing and reviewing medical information, celebrity contact with fans, and all the other opportunities to capitalize on the voice of the public through blogs.

In its simplest form, a blog is a Web log in which one writer publishes an opinion or point for discussion. Others respond to the initial blog statement, and then still others respond to the responders so that the "log" of comments and replies continues until sometimes the original point has evolved into something entirely different. More sophisticated blogs add links to others and become a network of discussion and information sharing. Depending on the credibility and popularity of the sponsor of the blog, it can, in effect, become a rival to more traditional sources of information and wield tremendous influence over its readers.

The power of blogs lies in their capability to challenge the role media conglomerates play in how information is delivered, phrased, reported, or otherwise distributed. The perspective of the reporter, station owner, and network can color the facts to sway the audience. The mere selection of what to report, broadcast, or distribute and what to omit shapes what the public knows. Blogs represent a number of communication technology innovations that will continue to alter the information flow.

A brief overview of the top six big media reveals how, through diversified holdings, a single media corporation can control the flow of entertainment, information, advertising, and Internet access:

TIME WARNER — The largest media conglomerate in the world owns The WB television network, CNN and its subsidiaries, Home Box Office (HBO) and its subsidiaries, Cinemax and its subsidiaries, Cartoon Network, Pay-per-view, TBS and TNT, American Online (AOL) and its subsidiaries, Allpolitics.com, Mapquest, Moviephone, Netscape, and Weblogs, to name a few. Time Warner products are also Warner Bros. Entertainment Group and its subsidiaries, The Atlanta Braves Major League Baseball Team, Synapse Group Inc. Marketing Company, Targeted Media, Inc., and Southern Progress Corporation which publishes *Southern Living At Home* magazine.

GENERAL ELECTRIC — GE owns NBC Networks/Production/Distribution and Programming, which includes thirty-eight television stations in two markets plus A&E, History Channel, Bravo, Mun2TV, SciFi Channel, Telemundo, Trio, USA, Universal HD, and Weather Plus. Several of these have international presence. In film and distribution, GE owns Universal Pictures, 80 percent of NB Universal, Focus Features, Rogue Pictures, and Universal Studios Home Entertainment. They have online holdings with NBC.com, MSNBC.com, CNBC.com, ivillage.com, Scifi.com, msn.com, and telemundo.com. They publish *SciFi Magazine*, produce equipment for the military, and are well known for their consumer electronics, financing, health care, and transportation.

WALT DISNEY — Disney owns ABC television network and its subsidiaries, ESPN and its subsidiaries, The Disney Channel and its subsidiaries, SOAPnet, Touchstone Television, and Lifetime and its subsidiaries. Disney also owns ten television stations in ten markets and an estimated fifty-two radio stations. Magazines, music, and book publishing associated with Disney are Buena Vista Music Group and Buena Vista Magazines. Big picture holdings are Walt Disney Pictures and its subsidiaries, Touchstone Pictures, Miramax Films, Hollywood Pictures, Buena Vista International, Home Entertainment and its subsidiaries, and Pixar Animation Studios.

NEWSCORP – NewsCorp owns FOX and its subsidiaries, thirty-seven U.S. stations in twenty-eight markets, satellite television's DirectTV, a host of international presence via satellite, *Big League, InsideOut*, News America Marketing, *SmartSource* iGroup magazines, *New York Post* newspaper, HarperCollins Publishers, ReganBooks, Fox Filmed Entertainment, and 20th Century Fox Films Corporation and its subsidiaries. Most of these have online presence.

CBS – With Leslie Moonves as CEO, CBS owns its television network and its subsidiaries, including The Movie Channel and its subsidiaries, Flix, Showtime and its subsidiaries, Sundance Channel, Infinity Radio, Inc., and its subsidiaries including an estimated 178 radio stations, and Simon & Schuster's family of publishers. Most of these have online presence.

VIACOM – Before splitting from CBS, Viacom was one of the largest media companies in the world. It still owns Music Television (MTV) and its subsidiaries, Nickelodeon and its subsidiaries, Paramount Comedy, The Box, Game One, BET and its subsidiaries, Viva, The Music Factory (TMF), Famous Music Publishing, Director's Cuts Production Music, Paramount Pictures, DreamWorks SKG, and iFilm Corp.

Although still in its infancy, blogging represented by sites like the Drudge Report that seem void of political gain strike a balance in journalism. The potential for every member of the American public to launch, or at least participate in, blogging communities poses a challenge, if not a direct threat, to these traditional media sources. The twin forces of access to the Internet and the public's sense of the right to participate through free speech are rapidly changing the nature of personal, cultural, and political communication. Blogs could develop into a seventh major force in communication distribution and influence.

Now the big six, as well as corporations, government, religious organizations, political parties, and ethnic groups not only recognize but also incorporate blogs into their communication. "Blog reports," making blogs themselves the news, can be seen on CNN and other news outlets. Professional blogging staffs now support major political candidates and office holders, scanning the blog communities for favorable and negative reaction and finding ways to take advantage, even by altering, influencing, or "spinning" the statements. "The bloggers are saying" echoes throughout broadcast news. Traditional institutions like universities now recognize blogs as no longer just subterranean chatter but significant enough to be reported in *The Chronicle of Higher Education*.

Although blogs have brought about a change in how many people get the hottest news or the facts and opinions that drive decisions, four major cautions should reverberate in our minds as we read and write blogs:

> **Blogging is a creative outlet**. Most blogs likely begin with the desire for personal expression and the joy of freedom from any restrictions. This unfettered speech can be cathartic, whimsical, literary, acerbic, racist, and even crude or pornographic. The nature of "creativity" varies with each writer. Embellishment, poetic license, and outright exaggeration or falsehoods surface in blogs. Personalities and the "voice" may even be in disguise.

Blogs must be recognized and read as personal creative writing. In all the ways we would apply common sense to judging any person we meet, we should approach blogs with caution.

Blogging is a more conversational version of broadcasting the news or viewpoints. In conversation, we communicate best when we talk to others who know us well and know how to interpret our familiar patterns of language. In the context of our "community," we can be ourselves and not fear judgments. Blogs have that quality of projecting a personality through a conversational style and offering a group discussion in which all share some affinity or intense interest in a particular subject. The red flag goes up when we fail to note that the engaging personality has overshadowed the lack of factual information or that the diatribe against some public or private figure has crossed the line of fair criticism.

The blogging community has prompted a major change in journalism. Blogs and bloggers as sources, bloggers scrutinizing journalists and their sources, bloggers "breaking" news, and journalists as bloggers are all shifts that reveal the impact on journalism. Perhaps one of the most significant and most basic advantages of blogs is simply the capability of any person mentioned in traditional media to respond. To be heard, bloggers do not have to get their message through the gatekeepers of major media outlets; they can respond from their personal computers and distribute their reply to as many people as are interested.

Blogs do not subscribe to checks and balances of ethics and quality control. Whatever interpretive slant major news operations may create, bloggers face little if any restriction, monitoring, or editing of what they write.

No mandated ethical or quality oversight or controls exist for blogs, and the degree of responsible monitoring resides with the sponsor of each blog. Legal challenges surface *after* damage to reputation, accuracy, and credibility have occurred. For those who become the subject of blogs, huge groundswells of support may be generated; for others, the effect can be devastating. The power of blogs is snowballing, and the responsible exercise of this form of free speech fosters ethical and legal questions.

Blogs provide a forum for a new breed of "citizen journalists" to supply real time eyewitness accounts of events around the world that the mainstream media does not, or cannot, cover and instantly communicate reports. In the case of increasing awareness about the plight of refugees in Africa—whether internal refugees in the Central African Republic or Darfurian refugees in Chad—sometimes only bloggers can continue the journalistic traditions.

The blogosphere supplies an outlet for whistle-blowers, soldiers in the field, and advocacy groups to disseminate information, increase public awareness, and create communities of like-minded individuals. Some offer journals about cancer care or other health issues and are designed to create support groups for difficult life journeys. In short, blogs are penetrating every facet of American life, and nowhere have they made more strides than in the political arena.

Who let the BLOGS out?

CHAPTER 2

BLOG COMES OF AGE:
The Election of 2004

> **BLOGGER'S CODE**: TAKE FULL RESPONSIBILITY FOR ALL ASPECTS OF YOUR BLOG, INCLUDING EVERYTHING THAT YOU POST AND THE COMMENTS YOU ALLOW.

In 2003, when Howard Dean announced that he was running for President, no one was more surprised than his mother. She told one magazine reporter, "I thought it was the silliest thing I'd ever heard." At the time, Dean had less than five hundred supporters and $100,000 in the bank.

One year later when his campaign came to an abrupt end, some said a "screeching" halt, Dean had raised $59 million. That amount was more than any Democrat in history. He succeeded in fundraising, using the most skillful application of the Internet ever employed in a political campaign. The blog had grown up and come a long way since the Drudge Report.

WHO LET THE BLOGS OUT?

The coming of age of the blog was the achievement of one of the unrealized promises of the 1990s about the Internet. Everyone with a computer and a modem had the potential to be a "digital Gutenberg." That dream was well on its way to fruition when the ".com Bubble" began to deflate. Ironically, the bubble burst just as some promising commercial software products were coming on the market that truly opened the door of personal publishing.

What had once been the exclusive domain of skilled programmers who knew HTML and other languages was immediately available to the typical computer user. No need to know any rules. A platform to the world was open to anyone with a Web connection. Publishing was as easy as pouring your thoughts into an empty text box and clicking a button. The barriers had been removed and not just for an elite few techies who knew a special code. Now blogging was for the masses.

THE BLOGS PENETRATE POLITICS

That politics was one of the first areas to experience major impact from the blogs was not surprising. As blogs became more popular, they began to exert a remarkable influence on the national political debate. Since the Internet is a relatively easy tool to use to amplify one's voice in the public square, anyone who has an opinion, time, and the technological ability to post a comment can participate.

Many political pundits and politically interested individuals have created their own blogs, in which they comment on candidates, campaigns, political trends, daily happenings, or other random musings. As the most open and democratic communications vehicle in history, blogging also operates without rules. Blog author Dan Burstein called blogging a marriage of "personality and attitude" with complex technologies, or "the raw human face of the brave new technological world."

Political parties at first adapted to the new technologies slowly and cautiously in an evolutionary manner. Political campaigns utilized the Internet to create static Web sites that contained information on the candidate and his or her policy positions. In essence, these Web sites were electronic extensions of campaign literature. State and federal parties also created their own to present information about meetings, candidates, and positions. These static sites reached a limited but growing number of politically interested people who were beginning to go online for their information.

USING THE INTERNET IN CAMPAIGN 2004

In the campaign of 2004, the Pew Research Center for People and the Press studied the use of the Internet. In their report, "The Internet and Campaign 2004," researchers found that in the year 2000:

- The overall number of political news consumers increased from 7 million in 1996 to 9 million in 1998 and to 34.5 million in 2000.

- Of the 34.5 million, 24 million used the Internet to research a candidate's policy positions.

- A total of 11 million news consumers researched a candidate's voting record online.

- Even more, 12 million participated in online polls.

- These Internet users were mostly between the ages of eighteen to forty-nine.

- They earned at least $30,000 per year and lived in urban or suburban areas.

- They had either some college or had graduated from college.

- Overall they continued to get their political news via television (70 percent).

- They used the Internet to get specific information (Pew, "The Internet and Campaign 2004").

From 2000 to 2004, there was a dramatic change in the habits of the electorate. The election of 2004 witnessed a sharp increase in Internet use by political campaigns, parties, and the electorate. By 2004, almost double the number (63 million) of people in 2000 used the Internet to get information about the elections. Statistically, they had the same as the previous demographic breakdown:

- Twenty-eight percent between the ages of eighteen and twenty-nine

- Fifty percent between the ages of thirty and forty-nine

- Nineteen percent between the ages of fifty and sixty-four

- Political Internet users continued to be primarily urban and suburban, with an increase in rural users from 17–21percent. (Pew)

During the 2004 election cycle, 63 million people used the Internet to research a candidate's policy positions, while 20 million researched a candidate's voting record. Their primary source of this information was online Web sites from traditional news sources—newspapers, television stations, cable news outlets—while 24 percent of the 63 million political Internet users went to alternative sources of information. These include campaign and party Web sites, issue-oriented Web sites, sites devoted to politics, government Web sites, and blogs.

A new category emerged in the analysis: people who used the Internet to disseminate jokes about the election via e-mail. In 2002, eight million people used the Internet for this purpose, but in 2004, thirty-two million people did. In addition, in 2004, the chat room and blog phenomenon really took off. Six million people participated in online political chat rooms, while 4 million people donated money online, an amount double ($2 million) the 2000 election. In the 2004 cycle, more than 13 million people went online to participate in some form of campaign activity, whether donating, finding out about events, or volunteering (Pew).

BLOGS FIND A PERMANENT HOME—IN POLITICS

In the election of 2004, many candidates' grassroots supporters created their own blogs to support their candidates, spending countless hours on their behalf. Blogs proliferated with commentary and opinion about the presidential candidates, and there were abundant negative blogs against the presidential candidates. The blatant partisanship of the election gave rise to particularly vitriolic forms of rhetoric even in traditional institutions.

The Democratic National Committee perhaps captured the spirit of the world of blogging by the title of their blog: "Kicking Ass: Daily

Dispatches from the DNC." In their blog, they explained why they believed that the blog was not an Internet fad:

> Blogs are popping up all over politics. Most of the Democratic candidates for president have added them to their Web sites.
>
> Why? What's so different about blogs that so many people have turned to them as a source of news and community? Is this just another Internet fad that will be nothing but a fond memory in a few years?
>
> We don't think so. One of the most common complaints about politicians and political parties is that there is no real communication between those of us in Washington and the rest of America.
>
> We put out press releases, e-mail letters, fundraising appeals, form letters, and advertisements. You write letters, volunteer, and donate.
>
> But where's the frank, one-on-one communication? Blogs make that possible. On Kicking Ass, you're going to meet real people at the DNC and hear real thoughts. And we're going to listen to you. ("About This Blog, Kicking Ass")

Although the Democratic National Committee failed to win the election, they certainly were correct in their forecast that blogging would not be an Internet passing fad.

THE HOWARD DEAN CAMPAIGN

Howard Dean, a Democratic presidential hopeful and former Democratic Governor of Vermont, integrated the use of the Internet into his overall communications, outreach, and fundraising strategy more thoroughly than any other candidate. He achieved stunning results.

Governor Dean's campaign manager, Joe Trippi, even wrote a book about this strategy, *The Revolution Will Not Be Televised: Democracy, the Internet, and the Overthrow of Everything*. Trippi and Dean applied basic campaign strategies to the virtual world of the Internet, creating a new paradigm for political campaigns. Trippi in *Blog* attributed much of the success of the approaches used in the Dean campaign to the evolution of the Internet. He said later, "I think the Net finally reached maturity."

In February 2003, Trippi joined the Dean campaign, and he used every resource the Internet had to offer in the election. He organized the grassroots support through Meetup.com. Through this online link, Dean supporters could contact each other and organize fund-raising events. In the month of September 2003, forty thousand people held 664 events across the United States. With competent Web staff support in Dean's headquarters, thousands of people donated millions of dollars in amounts of less than $100 each.

Public relations and development professionals understand how to leverage events and news items to the advantage of a client. Learning from the online advocacy organization MoveOn.org, Trippi created "news-pegged fundraising appeals" that were sent to an ever-expanding e-mail list whenever an "event" happened. These appeals—much like direct mail letters—sought to expand Governor Dean's grassroots fundraising base and reach new donors who gave small amounts to the campaign. Events could be a speech or comment by the opposition, a news article or story or a development on the domestic or international scene.

In addition, the Dean campaign leveraged existing technology of MeetUp.com, a company that facilitates people with common interests holding online discussions or meetings. The Dean MeetUp population eventually constituted a virtual mid-sized city, with several hundred thousand activists situated across the nation and beyond.

BLOG FOR AMERICA

One of the most successful aspects of Governor Dean's online campaign was the use of blogs. In 2003, the Dean campaign posted 2,910 blog entries on its "Blog for America" and received 314,121 comments, which were also posted. However, the campaign did not stop with this virtual discussion. It called for action in the non-virtual world. Targeting potential participants in the Iowa Caucuses and New Hampshire Primary, people who commented on the Blog for America then sent 115,632 handwritten letters to eligible voters.

Moreover, the Blog for America's homepage listed hundreds of other blogs as links. Two of those blogs also called for action in the non-virtual world. Deanyboppers clipped articles for major newspapers, thus becoming a research arm, and Dean Defense Forces organized calls to radio talk shows to "correct" what it perceived as unfair news coverage.

FREE DISCUSSION OF ISSUES

Howard Dean was the first political candidate to put up a blog in an election and no doubt exhibited a great deal of courage to risk the kind of attacks that can be associated with some of the more unsavory blogs. In an online discussion with Joe Trippi, Dean's campaign manager, an individual asked whether the campaign chose what commentary goes up on the blog or "is it really open for free discussion?" Trippi offered this explanation:

> It is open for free discussion. I have seen a lot of comments on other blogs that we monitor it and take some stuff down, but that is just not true.
>
> On occasion we take down profanity and things that are just too over the top. In fact now we have so many comments that I am sure that there is stuff that someone has posted that we haven't even seen yet.
>
> In the early days we had a guy that would come on and say "Howard Dean sucks" for pages. We would take it down because you would have to scroll forever to see anything interesting.
>
> Even now some stuff gets by us, but we try to let everyone post. Negative comments that are challenging or questioning Dean are left up all the time.
>
> It is only when they are super obnoxious that we have taken it down and that happens very rarely. (*Washington Post*, August 27, 2003)

Perhaps the greatest irony is that blogs, which played such an import role in the rise of Howard Dean, also played a significant role in his demise as a candidate. In fact blogs, magnified by the power of the Internet, served as a kind of echo chamber of the infamous "Dean Scream" and helped sink the presidential hopes of Howard Dean.

ONLINE DEMOCRACY

Overall, the Dean campaign's innovations adapted advocacy, fundraising, and grassroots strategies to the Internet. It created communities of like-minded people who were motivated to participate in its online discussions and activities. The Dean online campaign encouraged its participants to recruit new members. It gave the online activists something meaningful to do in the non-virtual world. They became part of a greater movement throughout the country. Finally, the Dean campaign held online referenda on major decisions—like whether or not to accept public campaign funds—thus giving the power to the activists. Many of these Internet innovations were adopted by the Bush and Kerry campaigns, as well as their respective party organizations.

Grassroots democracy was also a key feature of the Internet application in the Dean campaign. In November 2003, the Dean campaign held an Internet vote. It asked its supporters whether it should opt out of the federal campaign fund-raising system or turn over all its fund-raising to the grass roots organization. The result was that 700,000 people voted to tell Dean to opt out of federal funding. This was a historic vote. Dean became the first Democrat to opt out of the federal funding system.

MORE INNOVATIVE INTERNET TACTICS

In 2004, another innovation in the way the Internet was used by political campaigns was "micro-targeting." By using consumer data, the Bush-Cheney 2004 campaign was better able to target potential supporters and voters in key states, districts, and precincts. Bush-Cheney 2004 transmitted that information from its national headquarters to the field staff to inform the grassroots campaign strategy. This innovation gave Bush-Cheney 2004 a technological advantage over the Kerry campaign, even though many of the bloggers and Web sites on the left were highly motivated in their effort to unseat President Bush.

Online video made an appearance during the 2004 campaign, as well, with the Web site jibjab.com. It really broke through during the general election due to the use of online video clips by Swift Boat Veterans for Truth, the anti-Kerry 527 organization. The online buzz about the Swift Boat ads led to increased viewers online. Web-based videos were a secondary phenomenon, with blogs still the main innovation.

CITIZEN JOURNALIST

During the 2000 campaign, the primary source of political news continued to be the mainstream news organizations and their online Web sites. In 2004, the professional journalist had a new competitor on the news scene: the "citizen journalist." Now anyone with a point of view and a laptop could create his or her own Web log. Once established, this blog would become a source for other blogs—especially if they were linked on homepages. Many of these bloggers with catchy online names obtained press credentials for campaign events and the national party conventions. They would post their analyses as fact without regard for professional journalistic sourcing, ethics, or standards. Indeed, many of these political blogs were nothing more than opinion pieces, barely attaining even minimum standards of credibility.

Nevertheless, the blogosphere had a tremendous impact on established news media. Not only were the bloggers watching the established media for how a story might be shaded or presented, but the conventional news outlets were watching the bloggers for story ideas and information. While some blogs gained positive reputations among journalists, professional political analysts, and the public, many gained popularity specifically due to their viewpoint and sensationalism. As the latter blogs grew in readership, the influence on public opinion of their chat rooms, blog comments, and postings increased.

Nothing signaled the coming of age of the blog as an established communication medium among the major big media players like Election Night 2004. Everything good and bad about blogs was on display that night. NBC invited a handful of bloggers and Web pundits to spend the evening near the NBC election war room so they could be interviewed about the widening role of the Internet in the 2004 election.

They had among their guests Ana Marie Cox, the grand dame blogger of the gossipy Washington, D.C., blog called Wonkette. She posted her political prose from what she called the "NBC blogger's café" in Rockefeller Center. She said the whole ordeal was like being "denied your lithium prescription."

As for the world of blogs, it showed its muscle through numbers. On election day, the Drudge Report pulled in nearly 1 million visitors to its site. That was 30,000 more than the 964,000 people the *New York Times* drew to its Web site. Blogspot.com which cumulates thousands of Web journals as a host drew 330,000 readers, and many of these blogs were written live from the laptops of bloggers in campaign headquarters across the country.

How well the blogger citizen journalists performed during the election of 2004 is a matter of some dispute. Matt Drudge, sometimes called the "blog-father of the Web publishing movement," covered the election for his blog. About 2:00 p.m. on Election Day, he leaked exit poll data favorable to Senator John Kerry: "Kerry in striking distance—with small lead—in Florida and Ohio." Publishing exit poll data before the polls have closed is considered one of the sacred cows of the mainstream media, and bloggers violated this standard repeatedly during the election. And paid for it. Hundreds of bloggers turned out to be dead wrong with their "scoops." As Ana Marie Cox observed about blogger citizen journalistic powers, "all of a sudden blogs were back to being the pajama clad amateurs."

THE ELECTION IS STILL BEING FOUGHT BY BLOG

One of the blog's most tenacious characteristics is its ability to maintain an issue or point of view in cyberspace until the topic is absolutely exhausted. Blogs continued heatedly to fight the 2004 election well into the 2006 election campaign season. In 2006, Rollingstone.com carried a posting from Robert F. Kennedy Jr. entitled, "Was the 2004 Election Stolen?" It exhibits the type of oppositional partisanship that fueled the blog world during and after the 2004 Election.

ROBERT F. KENNEDY JR.
Posted Jun 01, 2006 5:02 PM

Like many Americans, I spent the evening of the 2004 election watching the returns on television and wondering how the exit polls, which predicted an overwhelming victory for John Kerry, had gotten it so wrong. By midnight, the official tallies showed a decisive lead for George Bush—and the next day, lacking enough legal evidence to contest the results, Kerry conceded. Republicans derided anyone who expressed doubts about Bush's victory as nut cases in "tinfoil hats," while the national media, with few exceptions, did little to question the validity of the election. The *Washington Post* immediately dismissed allegations of fraud as "conspiracy theories," and The *New York Times* declared that "there is no evidence of vote theft or errors on a large scale."

What is most anomalous about the irregularities in 2004 was their decidedly partisan bent: Almost without exception they hurt John Kerry and benefited George Bush. After carefully examining the evidence, I've become convinced that the president's party mounted a massive, coordinated campaign to subvert the will of the people in 2004. Across the country, Republican election officials and party stalwarts employed a wide range of illegal and unethical tactics to fix the election. A review of the available data reveals that in Ohio alone, at least 357,000 voters, the overwhelming majority of them Democratic, were prevented from casting ballots or did not have their votes counted in 2004—more than enough to shift the results of an election decided by 118,601 votes.

Over the course of the 2004 presidential campaign, the Internet would play a decisive role in attracting and mobilizing grassroots activists, spreading information on a candidate or the opposition, facilitating campaign fundraising, and recruiting volunteers for traditional grassroots activities. That role did not stop even after the election ended.

527 GROUPS

In addition, advocacy campaigns by 527 groups fed the Internet activity. The Center for Responsive Politics defines 527s as "tax-exempt organizations that engage in political activities, often through unlimited soft money contributions. Most 527s . . . are advocacy groups trying to influence federal elections through voter mobilization efforts and so-called issue ads that tout or criticize a candidate's record. 527s must report their contributors and expenditures to the IRS, unless they already file identical information at the state or local level."

As 527s, groups such as MoveOn.org posted assertions that companion e-mails would be sent to a list of friendly bloggers and grassroots activists. The activists would pass along this information to their personal e-mail lists, while the bloggers would post the assertion on their blogs as facts.

These 527s represented a variety of viewpoints and advocated on a diverse set of issues. They produced television and radio commercials, print advertising, Web sites, and advocacy literature mailed directly to homes. The dimensions of their activities were greater than in previous elections due to the heated nature of the political discourse during the election, as well as being an unintended consequence of McCain-Feingold Campaign Finance Reform. According to the Center for Responsive Politics, during the 2004 election cycle, these were the top spenders:

- Americans Coming Together - $78,040,480

- Media Fund - $57,694,580

- Service Employees Union - $47,695,646

- Progress for America - $35,631,378

- Swift Boat Veterans and POW's for Truth - $22,565,360

- MoveOn.org - $21,565,803.

The online, virtual world impacted the public debate on issues and candidates during the 2004 election cycle in a way that previous technological innovations had not. Due to its nature of being a free and open forum for exchange of ideas and information, the burden of critical evaluation moved from the originator of the information to the receiver. While traditional news organizations have editors, style manuals, and objective reporting standards, blogs do not necessarily have the same oversight structure. Yet, blogs often are treated with the same weight and in the same manner as traditional news outlets, leaving open the possibility that a person's opinion—no matter how extreme and unrepresentative of the majority of the electorate—can motivate others to impact the outcome of an election.

BEYOND MEDIA SPECTACLE

As bloggers were coming of age, they tended to be identified by their ability to generate a media spectacle, particularly around exposing something. "Oppositional Politics and the Internet," an article by Richard Kahn and Douglas Kellner, highlighted some of bloggers most prominent successes. Political bloggers played a significant role in focusing attention upon the racist remarks of Speaker of the House Trent Lott after the *Washington Post* had downplayed the incident. Bloggers set upon the *New York Times* over the Jason Blair plagiarism incident, not letting go until an executive editor resigned. U.S. prisoner abuse in Iraq with photographs posted on blogs launched a long-running quest to pin responsibility on soldiers and higher U.S. military authorities.

Blogs have now gone in many directions beyond mere spectacle. So-called "Watchblogs" focus on the media, specific reporters, specific newspapers, dissecting everything, uncovering their spin, and finding mistakes. Wireless bloggers cover major conferences. One wireless blogger and tree sitter, an environmentalist, is reported to have broadcast a wireless account of her battle against the Pacific Lumber Company from atop a large Redwood.

Given the explosion of blogging in many directions, it is almost impossible to get our arms completely around the movement. It is too big. Author Biz Stone, one of the earliest bloggers, now defines the magnitude this way:

> Blogging is self-expression, personal publishing, a diary, amateur journalism, the biggest disruptive technology since e-mail, an online community, alternative media, curriculum for students, a customer relations strategy, knowledge management, navel gazing, a solution to boredom, a dream job, a style of writing, e-mail to everyone, a fad, the answer to illiteracy, an online persona, social networking, resume fodder, phonecam pictures, or something to hide from your mother. (*Who Let the Blogs Out?*)

Whatever it is, most agree that a permanent feature of our culture has arrived.

BLOG TRENDS AND FORECASTS

In *Blog*, Kline and Burstein discuss a number of trends throughout their book that they see in the future of the blog. Innovations leading to the next generation of the Web center on the blog, especially those clustering around personalization. The attitude and personality reflected in blogs counter the assumption that technology depersonalizes communication and alienates individuals. Blogging promotes diverse voices and ideas; it becomes a metaphor for interactivity, community-building, and genuine conversation, sometimes one-to-one, often one-to-many.

Beyond the personal, the authors predict that blogging and the media will coexist and "cross-fertilize" each other. Business will take advantage of blogging in global customer segmentation and service, and blogging will continue to play an ever-evolving role in politics. As with all technology, the authors assume a long period of constant change.

THE SECOND SUPERPOWER

The blogging phenomenon that characterized the election campaign of 2004 is an example of what has been called by James F. Moore of the Harvard Berkman Center for Internet and Society as "the second superpower." This term refers not to a political entity but to the collective social force of an enlightened citizenry all over the globe, using their conscious power collectively to invent, act, and change the world. Moore recognizes bloggers as key citizens of this second superpower because of their ability to conduct real time dialogue about world events.

No matter what name we call the bloggers, they are "like a mind constituted of millions of inter-networked neurons." What they do can be called everything from "mass collaboration" and "customer-created content" in business to "smart mobs," the "wisdom of crowds," and "citizen journalists" in society as a whole (Moore and Berkman). The effect of the mass collaboration is powerful and stunning, and at times regrettable.

*". . . then shortly after that, my popularity
plummeted at the polls!"*

CHAPTER 3

BLOG AS POLITICAL WEAPON:
IRRESPONSIBLE FREE SPEECH

> **BLOGGER'S CODE:** ELIMINATE CONTENT THAT IS LIBELOUS, DEFAMATORY, KNOWINGLY FALSE, OR THAT MISREPRESENTS ANOTHER PERSON.

If the Election of 2004 proved anything about blogs, it demonstrated without a doubt their ruthless effectiveness in oppositional politics. What was not so apparent in 2004 is that blogs would become as ruthless inside political parties as they are when parties are arrayed against each other. The major contributing factor to this oppositional dynamic is that blogs post their analyses as fact without regard for professional journalistic sourcing, ethics, or standards. Indeed, many political blogs pass for fact when they are, in reality, nothing more than opinion pieces, barely attaining even minimum standards of credibility.

My own political experience provides a case study of how the political opposition used blogs to spread unverified information on my candidacy with reckless disregard of ethics to achieve their own political ends. It reveals the precise methods used by bloggers to spread information about a candidate or the opposition. It occurred at a time when I was considering running a write-in campaign for the 22nd Congressional District seat once held by Tom DeLay. This example reveals much about the powerful functional relationship between oppositional politics and blogs.

MY EARLY POLITICAL EXPERIENCE

In 2001, I entered Texas politics, and my experience was at first very rewarding. There was an easy and simple next-step feel to my progression from recognized community volunteer to new city council representative. My campaign was organized around my family's kitchen table; seasoned local political veterans were happy to stop by with advice for our fledgling staff of family and friends. Creating yard signs, developing a mailing list, organizing receptions in neighbors' homes, and recruiting volunteers was fun. In May 2001, I received 82 percent of the votes versus my opponent to win the opportunity to represent District 4 on Sugar Land's City Council.

Once on the Council, I gained important perspective on the management of our city and the people who wielded the greatest influence over the governance and future direction of Sugar Land. I decided to run for mayor the next year, and I upset a three-term incumbent when I earned 54 percent of the votes. Since 2002, I have been privileged to serve as mayor of this thriving, culturally diverse, and economically balanced city. Much of the experience has been personally rewarding. I've worked with some exceptionally talented people to create economic and social breakthroughs that have benefited the entire community, and I have made lifelong friends along the way.

But these successes have come at a personal cost. Those who power the engine of the political machine here in Fort Bend County have taken, and continue to take, their best shots at me in order to smear my reputation and attempt to sideline me from public office. Blogs and op-ed pieces—served up as fact—have been, at best, a distraction and at worst, an outright attack on me, my wife, and my daughters.

BULLDOZED BY THE BLOGS

In 2006, I was considering the next step in my political career, but blogs in a systematic effort to undermine my objectives blindsided me. These ferocious blog attacks were an oppositional response to my ambitions and require background to understand. The conflict goes back over a six year period to my initial election as mayor.

I've always believed that in local government we should first listen to our citizens, set goals and objectives to meet these needs we've identified, and work hard to accomplish these goals. Once a strategy is in place, elected officials must make a conscientious decision to work together and collaborate with the city manager and staff for the benefit of the entire community. This, of course, is Civics 101.

In the event that any of the constituency groups is not completely aligned with the strategy, we must do our best to understand the differences, acknowledge them with an eye toward achieving consensus, and always treat each individual's opinions with respect. Let's just call this Common Courtesy 101.

However, during my first year on city council, I got an insider's view to a style of governing that I did not anticipate. What I witnessed from a handful of council members—including our mayor—seemed more self-serving than I expected from public servants. I witnessed an attempt to usurp the city manager's authority and a prevailing arrogance that was akin to schoolyard bullying toward those whose opinions differed from their own. This was a recipe for disaster and undermined the authority and respect of the city's chief executive officer, the city manager.

SETTING THE STAGE FOR OPPOSITION

Emboldened to renew a collaborative and respectful spirit to Sugar Land's government, I decided to throw my hat in the ring and run for mayor. However, when I filed my application at 4:55 p.m. on the last filing day of the election cycle, this was perceived by some as firing the first shot across the bow of a military vessel. Granted, I didn't bother to ask the mayor—or his supporters within the Fort Bend Republican Party infrastructure—for permission to run against him. But I felt that our community deserved something better; Sugar Land deserved a leader who would listen to its citizens, embrace its rich diversity, and attempt to return to a more respectful approach of management-by-motivation versus management-by-fear.

For readers who are not in politics, let me share a slice of what it can be like. A person stands behind you at a public event and in a whisper says, "You have my support, but I can't be seen helping you . . . in case you lose the election." I cannot tell you how many people during the 2002 mayoral campaign told me that they'd vote for me but could not offer their public support for fear of retribution.

In the end, the support materialized, and it was as if an entire community had been set free from tyranny. In the polling booths, I won the election against the three-term incumbent mayor with 54 percent of the votes. But little did I realize at the time that winning this election would set into motion a take-no-prisoners style of blood sport politics and political paybacks that has since plagued Fort Bend County. Since then, this small group of angry local politicos has taken every opportunity to discredit, smear, and vilify me both personally and professionally.

THE OPPOSITION ATTACKS MY PROFESSIONAL WORK

As an example, I have spent twenty-five years representing investors in the acquisition, management, and turning-around of troubled businesses. In short, I buy troubled companies, recapitalize them, work with management, and attempt to breathe new life into what are often sick and dying companies. My goal is to fix failing businesses and save jobs. Sometimes I am successful, but there are times when the companies are too far gone for resuscitation. Most industry experts and venture capital/turnaround investment funds are content if their success rate is over 50 percent. In fact, a simple rule of thumb in the turnaround industry is that one-third of the investments will be a loss, one-third will be a break-even, and one-third will be wildly successful. My detractors have had a heyday with the nature of my business, misrepresenting facts, and painting a picture of a guy who bankrupts any business with whom he associates. One blogger said, "I worked for Emergency Networks, the company David Wallace ran into the ground. He has neither ethics, integrity, nor conscience." Not only is this misleading, it is also a boldfaced lie in many respects.

During the past twenty-five years, I have been involved with the purchase of over one hundred companies, and a full third of these companies were insolvent or bankrupt at the time I acquired them or was asked to get involved. When I arrive on the scene, I am almost always faced with a management team that is defeated and an investor group, or lenders to the company, that have achieved what I refer to as "investor fatigue," ready to pull the plug of the company's life support system. I buy other people's problems. But my detractors seized upon these business problems to attack me in blogs. One blogger responded to a posting with this comment, "I worked very closely with Dave at one of the companies listed. You hit the nail on the head; he is pure evil."

A good turnaround specialist continually faces attitudes like this in his job. He must embrace the management team, keep a clear head, give a brave smile, and demonstrate how all of us as a team are going to charge up this hill and win the battle. That is the confidence that the lenders, the creditors, the employees, the customers, and everyone expect from this specialist. Obviously, not everyone sees it this way because a successful turnaround is often accompanied by a reduction in overhead, a termination of contracts, or, in its worst case, many creditors being financially impaired. Of course, these people are upset and many times voice their displeasure about being negatively affected.

MY BUSINESS EXPERIENCE AIDED MY PUBLIC SERVICE

Turning businesses around, my chosen field of work, has been invaluable in my public service. Serving as mayor of a city is similar to managing a turnaround. People elect their officials to do good things. They expect positive results. When taxes are lowered, crime is reduced, and the economy improves, you don't receive many calls of congratulations. You're just doing your job and meeting expectations. Yet when a problem arises, we quickly hear from constituents who want to know how and when the problem will be solved.

Even though I am able to draw on my work experience for the benefit of the city, my detractors continually use my line of work to discredit me and raise doubt in the public's mind. After all, how can this man run a city when he cannot even run one simple business? They point to the "failed businesses" I have invested in or acquired. In fact, a tactic of fear was used in a blog message that if I was elected mayor, I would put the city of Sugar Land into bankruptcy.

This message is the same as if I said that you shouldn't vote for my opponent since he has been involved in over four hundred lawsuits, a fact that makes him sound unsavory, untrustworthy, and unsuitable for mayor. If he had been the defendant in all cases, perhaps the assumption would be sound, but if he is a lawyer representing clients, he is merely doing his job. To say that he has been involved in over four hundred lawsuits is factual, but implying that he is the subject of all these lawsuits would be misrepresenting the truth. In the same way, a turn-around specialist would be expected to be involved with companies in bankruptcy.

Blogs are in a unique position to manipulate facts since they sweep the landscape from every angle. From an early age, we teach our children not to manipulate facts, and as a society we place great value in the character traits of honesty and integrity. In business and in everyday life, people don't hesitate to identify a lie when they hear it. But in politics, it is known as SPIN. A lie just sounds less offensive if it's referred to as SPIN.

In 2006, when I attempted to get my name on the ballot to serve in the CD22 congressional seat, SPIN was in abundance, and the blog was the technological weapon of choice. The enemies I created by running for mayor five years earlier rallied in an attempt to "bring Wallace down once and for all," as one blogger stated. My fellow Republicans spun a strategy based on a technological whisper campaign leading to an all-out character assault, designed to impugn my reputation. And once the words appeared in "black and white," they were disseminated as fact. After all, the words could now be footnoted with an Internet site as a source—so they must be true!

THE BEGINNING

It started with a news blog called fortbendnow.com. This Fort Bend Now news blog asserts that comments on its site are moderated. They report that they post all comments unless they are libelous, contain personal attacks, or are off topic. They ask that individuals who submit comments not use "crude language" in the "interest of civility" because "your parents or children may be reading." As you will see, the Fort Bend Now news blog fell far below its standards of civility and avoiding personal attack.

On August 8, 2006, Bob Dunn, news writer, posted an article with the headline "With Delay Done, Wallace Mulls a Write-In Run for Congress." The article reported that I intended to run for the Congressional District 22nd seat in the 2006 election and said I was considering running as a write-in candidate. In April, Tom Delay had announced his intent to quit Congress and move to Virginia, and a court decision left the GOP without an official candidate on the ballot, opening the way for write-in candidates. I seriously explored the possibility of a write-in campaign.

From the moment of this announcement, the opposition forces mobilized a fierce attack using the blogs. The first posted comment from a GOP precinct chair set the tone, "Speaking as a CD22 Precinct chair, let me offer my official reaction. No. NO. HELL NO!" Noting the attack, one person commented, "So what's with all the Dave-haters here anyway? Sugar Land seems to be run very well."

Another commenter posted, "Mayor Wallace is well liked and respected in the community. You are correct. Sugar Land is run very well. He has done a tremendous job for this city. I think the only 'Dave haters' (as you referred to them) are on this forum."

The Precinct Chair of District 22 got in the last word, "Given Wallace's history of dirty business dealings and petty corruption . . . I'm surprised that anyone would support Wallace. Frankly, he makes the Virginian [Tom Delay] look squeaky clean." Almost forgotten in the flurry of these comments was a word of caution from one reader. She said, "You have to keep an open mind when reading the posts on the forum/opinion section. It is open to everyone and anyone, and, while it is enlightening to hear all sides of every issue, sometimes it gets ugly."

THE CD22 PRECINCT CHAIR SITE

After the second major blog posting of the contest, things really became ugly in a way that was almost impossible to contain. One of the CD22 Precinct Chairs, who had charged dirty business dealings in the news blog, continued his assault through his own personal blog. The weight and magnitude of the innuendo, hint, and guilt by association of his blog proved unstoppable. In a blog posting, "Some INFO on David Wallace," the individual listed twenty-seven items over an eighteen-year-period of my life that he claimed involved "bankruptcy, multiple business failures, and accusations of impropriety including RICO violations."

RICO is, of course, a criminal statute dealing with corruption and racketeering charges created to go after Al Capone. Next they threw in a little bit of arms dealing, drug dealing, and other criminal activities to make it all sound even more sensational. In fact, I kept waiting for the blogs to start discussing how I was birthed by Aliens so that I could surely make the cover of the *National Enquirer*!

The blogger, the CD22 precinct chair, began his blog by explaining that folks had asked him why he believed David Wallace "to be unethical, corrupt, and unfit to represent the GOP" in the CD22 race. He ended his blog by going in for the kill. He took twenty-seven examples, tabloid news articles, opinions, court filings, and innuendo, and then he accumulated them into one overwhelming accusation. I have never once spoken with or met this man, yet he concluded his blog by comparing me to Tom Delay and wrote:

> "Now let's be real honest here—there may be perfectly logical and reasonable explanations for some of these items—but a reasonable person must wonder if such explanations exist for every single one of them, including the legal/business/financial issues that are currently at issue. And more to the point, do we really want to have a candidate with this much baggage following in the footsteps of our former congressman, whose ethical record has been questioned over the years—and who is currently facing criminal charges?"

Even one reader of the news forum found the whole process to be unsavory. "Asking for proof of an allegation," she said, "is just too much for you guys. Any allegation you make should be accepted as fact in your world." The reaction to the twenty-seven comments was swift and visceral in some cases, one blogger stating, "Wallace is a bullshitter and a scum bag. . . . He's red meat to the democraps. . . . If the republicans back him their [sic] fools, the DNC will enjoy a tasty lunch."

Many of these blog postings were "cut and pasted" into numerous documents and CDs and then were copied and distributed on numerous occasions via the Internet blogs, mail, and hand delivery as "truthful, fair and balanced, and factual" statements.

BLOGS FAIL TO UNDERSTAND THE TURNAROUND INDUSTRY

One of the great failings of the blogs in this situation is that they never attempted to provide a fair and balanced view of the nature of the industry I work in: turning around businesses that are in trouble. In every insolvent situation, by definition, I have jumped into a company where the assets are less than the liabilities. Many times I am encountering a situation where there has been mismanagement. Many times I have unions or other employee groups that are livid due to past practices, unfunded pensions, or unpaid benefits. And many times, I uncover things from prior management that are downright dishonest or illegal. Remember, I am dealing with a troubled situation when I arrive on the scene.

When fresh capital is being invested in a company, a prudent investor will not throw capital into a company and have their "new money" be repaid merely by digging out of a hole. Consequently, not all of the lenders, employees, and creditors will be happy with the plan of reorganization or workout strategy. It is a zero-sum game. When new money comes in, some changes need to occur.

Change in many cases is hard to accept. When employees are laid off, people complain. When lenders are told that they will not recover all of their money, they are not happy. When investors are told that their investment is worthless, they do not sit by quietly. Sometimes I can smooth these emotions and work out a settlement, and sometimes these folks yell or worse. They can sue the company or the new investor group.

Of course, nobody likes to deal with lawsuits. However, they are ever-present in corporate America and even more present in dealing with troubled companies. I am pleased that after all of the companies in which I have acquired, invested, represented, or formed—over one hundred in total—only a handful of lawsuits have been filed naming me as a defendant. Quite honestly, I would have expected many more and am proud of the fact that I was able to create an environment where people would approve the plan of reorganization, rather than attempt to fight or litigate the restructuring.

THE THATCHER FAMILY RELATIONSHIP

The blogs attempted to show that I was somehow tainted by an association with Mark Thatcher, the son of the former British Prime Minister. As for the Thatcher connection, I can say that I am truly honored to have been affiliated with Lady Margaret Thatcher. The people I met, the places I visited, and the things I learned under her leadership are invaluable to me today. From this former prime minister, I gained an insight into the workings of public-private relationships, a lesson in supply-side economics, and a keener appreciation for the overall economic impact that it can have on a country, state, and city. I personally witnessed over $27 billion in privatization take place in the United Kingdom while I was a business partner with the Thatcher family.

As the Founding Treasurer and Director of the Margaret Thatcher Foundation, I was exposed to many wonderful things throughout this entire world. To experience first-hand the millions of lives being changed as the world evolved from various communist regimes to countries of democracy and capitalism has forever changed my view of the world. The principles of freedom, democracy, and rules of law—as seen through the eyes of such a great world leader—is something I am truly fortunate to have experienced.

The British tabloids, which make the *National Enquirer* look like a conservative newspaper, have always had a stinger out for Mark Thatcher. I guess when they tired of attacking his mother, they went for her Achilles heel, which was clearly Mark. Consequently, the London journalists were always trying to sensationalize his business and personal life, which included me due to my friendship and business partnership with his family. I do find amusing that bloggers, in an attempt to quote what they think are legitimate news sources from the UK, are in actuality referencing tabloid articles.

The blogs also seem to do a very good job of linking business failures with personal financial challenges. In many ways, the more personal the financial challenge, the more enjoyment these writers have in their statements. This is a sad state, indeed, if people actually gain enjoyment out of witnessing the financial difficulties of others.

MY REAL FINANCIAL DIFFICULTIES

At the risk of spoiling their fun, the truth is that my family's personal financial difficulties are limited to two separate situations. The first was in the mid-1980s when I was in my early twenties and fresh out of college. After going to work for a real estate syndication company, I was rewarded, along with several other employees, with a bonus and granted the option to invest—at a discount—in unsold limited partnership interests. As we made these investments, we were told that we had to have "basis" in this investment and must guarantee the underlying debt of the properties. Being a young twenty-something, believing I was "bulletproof" at the time, having seen the real estate market on a continuous climb from the '70s into the '80s, and having the assurance that the company owners were also guaranteeing the debt, I decided along with the others to execute bank debt guarantees.

Unfortunately for my fellow employees and me, the real estate market plummeted, affecting many more people across Texas and nationwide. As I learned the tough lesson of "what goes up must come down," I saw the real estate values and my financial worth turn upside-down. These were some very difficult times, but the knowledge I gained in workouts and turnarounds was the foundation for what I would do for the rest of my life.

In the year 2000, the second financial difficulty happened when I had an investment company holding about forty separate companies. During a family trip to Phoenix, I went down to the hotel pool for my usual early morning workout routine. I remember walking into the pool and floating on my back, but the events that followed would change my life forever. I lost consciousness while I was in the pool, drowned, went into cardiac arrest, and was found flat on the bottom of the pool several minutes later.

Today, the miracle of my complete recovery is beyond my comprehension. I was in a coma and not expected to survive. For the next three months, I was in and out of hospitals, being tested and rehabilitated. Naturally, this significantly detracted from my ability to work. Given the financial challenge of funding my company and maintaining employees, I elected to wind down the company and spin off the various assets.

During the next several years following the drowning, I was successful at personally satisfying over $900,000 in obligations owed by me and my company. My near-death experience was humbling on a number of levels, most significantly spiritually, emotionally, and financially. The fact that writers of blogs find any humor at all in this experience is evidence enough that they don't have the facts. The truth is I am proud that I was able to satisfy these obligations. Even more than that, I am eternally thankful for the many wonderful people who prayed for and lifted my family through this difficult time. This sense of friends, neighbors, and strangers coming together to help someone in need is what eventually ignited my desire to serve my great community as a public servant.

Yet the bloggers get great joy out of spinning these financial difficulties in an attempt to raise doubts in people's mind about my financial acumen.

CHEROKEE INVESTMENT PARTNERS

The blogs also stated that I had a conflict of interest through "privileged information" as mayor with a company intending to develop real estate in Sugar Land. As for the questions of my integrity and the development in Sugar Land, let me shed some light on the facts regarding the redevelopment of the Imperial Sugar Company's original site constructed over one hundred and sixty years ago.

Searching for the right private partner to redevelop the Imperial Sugar property proved to be a challenging task. Each firm I approached, and there were several, struggled to develop an economically viable plan that addressed the site's environmental conditions and existing infrastructure while preserving our city's rich history. In June 2004, I attended the U.S. Conference of Mayors annual meeting and heard Tom Darden, the Chief Executive Officer of Cherokee Investments, speak about his firm's experience in repositioning "environmentally challenged" or "impaired" real estate. Cherokee Investments is the world's largest private organization that specializes in the acquisition, remediation, and sustainable redevelopment of brown fields.

After evaluating the redevelopment expertise and experience of many local and regional private developers, I determined that clearly Cherokee Investments' unique business model would be critical to the success of our project. Cherokee Investments' mandate to transform areas where urban blight and environmental contamination impede economic growth and development was right in line with Sugar Land's need. After I discussed the Imperial Sugar opportunity with Cherokee Investments, they visited the site and expressed a willingness to evaluate the property and its opportunities. If it proved consistent with the core capacities and investment strategies of Cherokee Investments, the firm would invest in a long-term partnership with the city of Sugar Land.

However, Cherokee Investments was looking for a local development partner. After being turned down by many, I looked to a guy whose family had been involved in the development of thousands of single family homes in the Houston area. As time went by, I decided to co-invest with this local developer on other real estate investments, none, of course, having to do with Imperial Sugar or Cherokee Investments. In the end, Cherokee Investments made the investment, I am no longer a partner with this local developer, and he is no longer involved with Cherokee Investments. The good news is that Cherokee Investments has closed on the Imperial Sugar tract and is now redeveloping a great community asset.

Nevertheless, after consulting with the city manager and in an abundance of caution, the city manager and I made the decision to create a "so-called" firewall to ensure that there was not even a perception of a conflict of interest. Again, the city manager and I made the decision. But once again, don't let the facts get in the way of a good SPIN.

My opponents chose blogs as their mode of communication to create a forum, and then take information gathered as alleged fact and attempt to disseminate the materials through various means. The strategy proved to be highly effective, but their SPIN was based, once again, on untruths and exaggeration.

One would normally think that a small group of individuals, no matter how vocal they might be, would not affect the outcome of an election. Yet the process of getting one's name on the ballot following DeLay's resignation was a selection process by four separate precinct chairs in Fort Bend, Harris, Brazoria, and Galveston Counties. Consequently, this was a very small universe of people that could be manipulated into believing the venom that was being spewed by these detractors. In essence, why would they not believe a handful of their fellow precinct chairs who are supposed to have the Republican Party's best interest at heart?

The fact is that every survey and poll conducted during that time revealed that in a general election only two people had enough name recognition to win the election. Those two people were Judge Robert Eckles and me. Robert had made it clear to me that he was not going to resign his post as Harris County Judge to run as a write-in, and I was prepared with a strategic plan to win as a write-in candidate. The White House and the National Republican Congressional Committee (NRCC) were apprised of these developments and were consulted by my political advisors at every step of this entire process.

Of course, this information was also shared with the leadership in the Texas Republican Party, but they seemed disinterested in what the pollsters were saying. Instead, they were intent on listening strictly to a handful of precinct chairs, the people who nominate and elect the leadership of the state's party infrastructure. And in this game, a small roomful of people made the decision to support Shelly Sekula-Gibbs in a write-in candidacy.

Knowing what the pollsters were saying about her inability to win as a write-in, I was faced with two choices. I could move forward and leave my name on the ballot as a write-in candidate. But never in the history of Congress has a write-in candidate won when there were more than two write-in candidates on the ballot. In short, if I stayed in the race, no Republican would have a chance, and I surely would have been blamed for the defeat. The other choice was to remove my name from the ballot and throw my support behind the other Republican write-in candidate.

I made the choice to remove my name from the ballot and support Sekula-Gibbs. I made this decision because I viewed it as being in the best interest of the Republican Party, especially since all of my polling intelligence pointed to her being defeated in the election. Even though she ultimately lost the race and the Republicans lost this seat in Congress, I feel I made the best decision.

When I look back on my whole experience of blogs over my proposed write-in campaign for the 22nd Congressional District of Texas, I am struck by a single major characteristic of the blogging world. By their very nature, there is no higher appeal of the information, charges, innuendo, or attacks that may be carried out in a blog. About the only way to appeal large volumes of misinformation in a blog is through the long, labor intensive process of starting your own blog as a counter measure. Few people have the time or money to make such an effort, so misinformation and innuendo are allowed to stand unchallenged. This hard-to-challenge aspect of blogs proves an advantage to those who are allowed to use them anonymously as political weapons and a disadvantage to those who have little recourse or defense.

ONE NATION UNDER BLOG—WHAT IF?

BLOGGING THE PAST

What if the British had been victorious in the American Revolution? What if Hitler had survived World War II? What if the United States stopped at the Mississippi River? What if the South won the Civil War? What if President Kennedy had not been assassinated? Questions like these lead us back in time to imagine how a different outcome for a single event or series of events would affect us today.

Writers and historians call this process "alternate history," and readers enjoy numerous books that reflect some aspect of this genre. For example, in *Ruled Britannia* (2002), Harry Turtledove, one of the masters of alternate history, speculates that in 1588, the Spanish Armada defeats the British Navy, leading to Catholic dominance in England with Elizabeth I imprisoned in the Tower of London. In *The Plot Against America* (2004), Philip Roth writes about a United States in which Charles Lindberg defeats Franklin Roosevelt in the 1940 Presidential election.

In *The Children's War* (2001), J. N. Stroyar joins a number of other authors in speculating what would have happen if the Nazis had won World War II. Turtledove shifted his focus to the Civil War with *A Novel of the Second War Between the States* (1997). His series of novels probes how the ambitions of men like Sam Clemens, Frederick Douglas, and Theodore Roosevelt would have been altered and would have reshaped American history as we know it.

Frequently overlooked wars and other significant moments take on new significance when catapulted into the historical limelight through an "alternate" treatment. In *1812: The Rivers of War*, for instance, Eric Flint changes the lives and perceptions of Andrew Jackson and Sam Houston so that the Trail of Tears did not occur and a multiracial republic was created in the South.

Mystery, science fiction, time travel, literary thrillers, fantasy, and nonfiction all transport readers to a world that would have existed if only events had worked out differently. Dan Brown's *DaVinci Code* generated world-wide interest and debate by appealing to the possibility of an alternate reality of Christianity. The popular *What If?* Series (1999–2003) edited by Robert Cowley and Robert Sobel's *For Want of a Nail: If Burgoyne Had Won at Saratoga* (1973) have attracted readers mesmerized with the possibilities of alternate history.

Robert Frost's "The Road Not Taken" brings the experience of choosing one path over another, to an intensely personal level. We all think about those key decisions when—in a moment of inspiration, intuition, or carefully plotted action—we took some road that forever changed our lives. If we had chosen another path, we can only speculate and imagine the consequences.

An interesting notion that feeds the popularity of asking "what if?" lies in the assumption that if any person on the earth at any moment in the past had changed one action, the current moment would not be identical to the present. The logical extension of this "alternate history" thinking prompts us to ponder how everything we do now will affect the future. How will the position we take, the vote we cast, the blog we write impact others and the outcome of significant events? If we assume that seemingly casual, even personal off-the-cuff comments and postings serve only to vent our strong feelings of the moment, we might take heed from the alternate history writers about the potential impact of relatively insignificant, often impetuous, actions.

From the earliest history of this country, the people's voices have influenced the outcome of key events. Debate, protest, and support have found their voice through the communication technology of the time.

Today blogs give more power to the public to express opinions than ever before. The responsible, and irresponsible, use of blogs and other forms of unfettered and unregulated electronic expression can have dramatic and long lasting effects. *One Nation Under Blog* focuses on the growing impact of blogs and how they might have changed the course of American history if the technology had been available throughout the last two hundred years.

Whether the qualifications and monarch-like demeanor of George Washington, the controlling nature of John Adams, or the Deism of Thomas Jefferson, the founding fathers would have likely been prime targets for blogs. Certainly the administrations of Abraham Lincoln and Ulysses Grant, associated with a conflict that galvanized the country, might have attracted millions of "hits." In the twentieth century, the accelerating pace of communication would have allowed blogs to reflect and perhaps influence the presidencies of Franklin Roosevelt, John Kennedy, and Lyndon Johnson.

We strive to understand the past so that we can make wise choices about how we influence the future. By imagining how blogs might have affected "what if?" in history, we challenge ourselves to consider prudently our actions that may alter the history we are now making for future generations.

"Not another King George?"

CHAPTER 4

BLOGGING THE FOUNDING FATHERS:
KING, DICTATOR, OR ENLIGHTENED DEVIL?

> **BLOGGER'S CODE:** OPERATE YOUR BLOG AS TRANSPARENTLY AS POSSIBLE, REQUIRING VALID E-MAIL ADDRESS FOR COMMENTS.

BLOG 1

The bungler is to blame for this fine mess we now find ourselves in. We should have secured a diplomatic solution to our dispute and not rushed to war. How on earth did this man—on whose head already lays the blame for hundreds of dead and wounded—how did he get elected and get command? — *Frankly Speaking*

BLOG 2

Believe me, I do not speak from whim or self-interest but from unfortunate experience. The snake has worked against the interest of freedom previously—always in the guise of what was best for the country. He sought to remove successful generals from command if they were not of his political stripe or if they were too successful. Without military experience himself, he has succeeded in emasculating our forces. He is not a patriot but a schemer. — *Military Man*

BLOG 3

We must understand the true nature of this election. Forces that seek control of our country threaten the moral

souls of our children and grandchildren. They display the hubris
of the devil himself. Elevating human intelligence over divine is
dangerous blasphemy and, in a President, fatal. — *True Christian*

If these postings by bloggers seem to echo the issues relevant in elections today, they do. If they appear to reflect the issues that generated debate when this country was founded, they are. If the conclusion is that politics remains much the same, just operating in a different time and technological environment, so be it.

Posting # 1 attacks George Washington and questions his qualifications as well as his capability as a military leader. Posting # 2 focuses on John Adams and questions his patriotism and steadfastness. Posting # 3 voices the concerns of religious citizens who opposed the Deism of Thomas Jefferson and feared that his disbelief in traditional Christianity would destroy the country. Variations of these issues still mark political debates even today.

Considering how blogs might have changed the course of this country's history gives us pause to think about the impact of those written today in the heat of political and personal battles over policy, values, and reputations. How would the presidencies and legacies of George Washington, John Adams, and Thomas Jefferson have differed if blogging communication technology and instant distribution of personal opinion had existed in the late eighteenth century? What if those blogs had altered history?

CAN HE LEAD? WILL HE BE KING?
BLOGGING GEORGE WASHINGTON

History is often written by the victors and sometimes reflects only that faction's point of view. George Washington is remembered as a great military hero and the "Father of Our Country." He was universally loved among those who served under his command, but the common soldier's view, or the common citizen's belief, does not always triumph in politics, war, or recorded history. In 1777, no one knew the outcome of the fight for independence. What seemed like a righteous response to British tyranny had turned into a long struggle with no quick end to the conflict. Confidence waned, husbands and sons died, and citizens questioned the wisdom of their leader.

IS HE QUALIFIED?
Gateway to Victory Blog

In yet another military fiasco, our current Bungler-in-Chief again led the courageous American Troops to disaster. A plantation owner, his only skill is to shepherd soldiers to slaughter as if they are livestock. His cowardly flights provide mercy for the troops under his so-called command, but his pretenses of courage inevitably lead to catastrophe. When will our people have enough bloodshed and slaughter? When will they replace this unqualified buffoon?

COMMENT # 1

The Bungler should be tried for mass murder and shot! His incompetence is surpassed only by his arrogance, recklessness, and fool hearty desire for battle! Many of my brothers in arms have been sacrificed under this Southerner's command, due only to the political corruption of our so-called representatives in the Continental Congress. When they play politics, New Englanders die. – *Soldier in the Field*

COMMENT # 2

Politics pure and simple. At this he is a master. Congress, in its infinite wisdom, put at the head of our militias a Virginian who has never demonstrated anything but a willingness to sacrifice the lives of our valiant troops in order to protect his family's business interests. In 1754, we from Virginia were sent to protect his family interests in the Ohio Company. Oh, what a disaster! – *Fed Up Fellow Virginian*

COMMENT # 3

Wait a minute, Fed Up. In 1754, I was there and witnessed your spineless whining about waiting until we were fully prepared—and likely dead. Our leader knew the terrain and the enemy, had exhausted diplomacy, and accepted terms of surrender only after you instigated a mutiny among the soldiers. When would have been the right time to engage—after our families and properties were taken? – *Virginian Veteran*

COMMENT # 4

You have already become a slave to the Mt. Vernon Monarch. Which position in his dynasty did he promise you? What is your current relationship with him? How will you profit from his ascent? – *Wary Citizen*

COMMENT # 5

We need to look no further for alternate leadership than General Horatio Gates. At Saratoga, the valiant general presided over the most valiant victory we have yet achieved. General Gates has informed us in Congress of his momentous victory—and he should be rewarded with overall command. We do not need any more retreats or losses. We need noble commanders to lead us to victory. – *Congressional Gatekeeper*

IN REALITY, in the late 1770s, these imagined blogs represent prevalent attitudes. Washington faced repeated challenges about his competence as a military leader. Throughout the war for independence, Congress considered calls for his replacement by its own representatives, including John Adams, Richard Henry Lee, Samuel Adams, and Roger Sherman. The Congressional faction supported General Gates' aspirations to become Commander-in-Chief of the military force. Washington's strongest supporters, however, remained the soldiers who fought under his command.

Washington insisted that Congress give General Gates a commission because he was an able leader. As Washington's rival, Gates cultivated his own support among troops and congressional delegates. As Paul Ford points out in *The True George Washington*, upon Gates' victory at Saratoga, he sent word directly to Congress and not to his commander-in-chief. Washington took this and other insults in stride, especially since he valued the contribution of General Gates to the cause of independence and needed his military expertise.

Washington became famous for his military pursuits during the French and Indian War. London newspapers featured stories about his military heroism and several letters by him. He understood that the traditional British military strategy would not succeed. Although his first military battle led to surrender, it was the only one in his long career.

THE ISSUES about responsible free speech reflected in these blogs still echo today. Anonymity allows critics to make charges without revealing the source. Eyewitness testimonials, without verification, can raise doubts about a target without any proof. Events from a person's past can be distorted and slanted to suit the writer's purpose. Negative comments seem to outnumber and outweigh positive postings, perhaps because blogging frequently grows out of the impetus to challenge an idea, position, or person. Favorable responses are often defensive and written not as the original blog, but as reactive postings.

WHAT IF George Washington did not retain his status as Commander-in-Chief of the revolutionary forces? What if one of the other generals had succeeded him? What if Washington had not remained as leader and inspired soldiers to serve despite harsh conditions and disheartening support from Congress? Could the impact of blogs have altered the outcome of the war for independence?

HAVE WE TRADED ONE KING GEORGE FOR ANOTHER?
MAN OF THE PEOPLE BLOG

 My friends, I have just come to our Capital City and am appalled at the scene that I witnessed. After our long struggle against the oppression and tyranny of the British monarchy and our subsequent fight to ensure that our Constitution reflected the true nature of democracy, I witnessed no less than a new, elected monarch! Our long struggle may have been in vain. Man of the people—I think not!

I witnessed our President traveling through the streets in a carriage—drawn by no less than six white horses. He holds himself as if he is exalted above the rest—even those of us he has asked to serve in his administration. His aristocratic demeanor was well known during the war, but the behavior that I witnessed today is a dangerous threat to the very fabric of our newly created Republic. We must not let this new type of monarchy become entrenched!

COMMENT # 1

I would beware of besmirching our President's actions or motives, for it is his unassailable reputation that is a primary value to our nascent democracy. His image and reputation give our United States a respect that we would otherwise not enjoy. Perhaps jealousy moves the Man of the People to make these disparaging comments—an emotion that is both dangerous and counterproductive. – *Frankly Speaking*

COMMENT # 2

Shouldn't we have a man of learning, educated in philosophy and rhetoric, to represent us, especially around the world? What we have is a self-taught man hesitant to participate in open debate and to carry the defense of democracy to our allies and our enemies. His regal pose will send the wrong message. – *Man of the People*

COMMENT # 3

We who love liberty above all else, who have shed our own blood and the blood of others, who have made sacrifice after sacrifice, will ensure that the dignity and ceremony do not translate to oppression and tyranny. My fellows, join me in this watch to ensure the longevity of our cause and liberty for future generations. – *Watchdog for Liberty*

COMMENT # 4

I know from experience that the humility of our president is no guise. Having the extreme honor of serving under his command for seven years, I can testify that he is the best and most honest man ever to grace God's good earth. He gives no quarter to those who seek personal gain and does not suffer cowardice. Our President is a man of the people. – *Virginia Veteran*

COMMENT # 5

We must elevate his reputation even further, for as his reputation soars, so does the country's. In a man of lesser character, caution would be advisable, but in this man, at this moment in establishing our nation's sovereignty, his demeanor and comportment suit our best interests. We can, and must, trust our future to him. – *Democracy's Guardian*

IN REALITY, Washington learned from the prior experience of the Presidents of the Continental Congress. They were treated as "first among equals" with the emphasis on equality. With the encouragement of John Adams, Washington sought to give the Executive Office the dignity of a Head of State. He realized that he should not imitate European monarchs but understood that he must maintain a level of decorum and even a reserved manner of silence that would allow him to impress world leaders. Perhaps his most important accomplishment remains his ability to rise above intrigue and criticism to establish the nature of the American Presidency—an office that had no parallel in history or politics—and the dignity with which the office is still regarded.

THE ISSUES about responsible free speech in these blogs reflect the uncertainties of a young nation and still permeate blogging today. When does the watchdog function cross a line to unfair personal attack? How does experience with a public figure in one realm of personal interaction cast a shadow or provide a defense in another? What is the balance between personal and public personas? Should bloggers consider their postings as voicing their feelings of the moment or as well-considered positions? How much of a blogger's comment can be accepted without knowing the real identity of the writer, his or her own character and experience, and what he or she has to gain by voicing opinions?

WHAT IF George Washington had accepted the status of the presidency as first among many without cultivating the image of a Head of State? Would the rest of the world eventually have accepted the United States as anything other than a temporary alliance of a group of states more separate than unified? Would John Adams have been able to present his credentials to the court of King George and be recognized instead of hanged as a traitor? What if the questions of Washington's qualifications had overshadowed the faith in his character? Could blogs have undermined the first Presidency?

HEIR APPARENT OR PRETENDER TO THE THRONE?
BLOGGING JOHN ADAMS

Nothing brings out the bloggers like the opportunity to attack an opposing political party's nominee. In 1796, the same situation existed in the election to choose the second President of the United States. Yet the American political system is known today for its peaceful transition of power between leaders and between parties. What we take for granted did not evolve without struggle, contest, and patriotism.

PERSONAL POWER MONGER?
Publius Blog

We are at a critical stage in the course of our new country, and we must beware of false patriots. Too late have I understood that we have a snake in our midst. We have the chance with this election to raise the question of malicious government and the question of rights. While our venerated President holds the respect of the populous, his Vice President does not. The self-styled inheritor would create a monarchical government, as he advised General Washington. Under the guise of "honor" and "dignity," he counseled the President to pretense and airs. We must ensure that this is not the last free election that our country faces.

COMMENT # 1

The lead candidate is not for us. He will turn his back on our faction and reverse our advances. We face the possibility of war within months of our next President's inauguration, and we must be prepared. Like the Republican Jefferson, the Vice President does not have the fortitude for waging war. He will stall, excuse, negotiate, and surrender instead of pursuing the rightful military course. We will capitulate our hard-won freedoms and independence due to his cowardice. Remember—he was talking while we were fighting. He will not change. – *Military Man*

COMMENT # 2

He runs in the front of the Federalist pack toward the Crown. As our Minister in London, he sought to arrange the betrothal of his son to the King's daughter! Worthy of European monarchal families, this action revealed his intent to create a new empire. What would he do if handed the full weight of government? It would be a short time before he would deliver us to the Crown. – *Guardian of Democracy*

COMMENT # 3

The Vice President is a master manipulator. I remember well his energy during the Continental Congress. Indeed, his activity far exceeded mere enthusiasm. Serving on ninety committees and chairing twenty, he sought to control all proceedings. He had a deep need to have a hand in every deliberation and to ensure that it went his way. From his speech and the ferocity of his debate, one might think that the whole enterprise of independence was his idea! – *Man of the People*

COMMENT # 4

Leadership from the South must be continued. Our beloved President's retirement should not be a signal for secession of our rightful role in leading the country. God has indeed smiled on our great Southern States, our commerce, and our society. It will not do to have either a Northerner misrepresent us or a Virginian whose very philosophy ensures the toppling of our way of life. There is but one true candidate, one loyal man, whose stock and experience will serve our purposes. – *Carolina Gentleman*

COMMENT # 5

Once again, I must caution the Federalist contingency. An honorable man, the Vice President has been chosen by the whole faction. We must be careful about destroying our unity with internecine fighting. Our differences are not of substance, and we must remember that there are greater threats to this young nation than the use of diplomacy. Rushing to war is never prudent, but always possible. My brothers, let us remember our dignity and put aside these petty differences lest we deliver the entire election to Jefferson himself. – *Pursuer of Justice*

IN REALITY, in 1796, the Federalist faction controlled all aspects of government: executive, legislative, and judiciary. Vice President John Adams and Thomas Pinckney of South Carolina were the candidates opposing Thomas Jefferson supported by Aaron Burr and the Democrat-

Republicans. Adams should have been the head of the Federalist Party, but Alexander Hamilton, using his moniker "Publius" from *The Federalist Papers*, challenged Adams for power and agitated behind the scenes.

This election refueled debates about states' rights, the strength of a centralized government, the power of an executive branch, a standing army, and a federal system of taxation. Factions, loosely organized groups of like-minded citizens, existed instead of political parties. Candidates did not campaign but retired to their homes while supporters vied for the attention of the few who really chose the President. The candidate with the most votes became the President, and the runner-up became Vice President.

Bloggers would have flourished in this environment because rumor, innuendo, accusation, and scare tactics were common. The uncovering of a plot by Hamilton and the endorsement of Jefferson by the French Ambassador shifted the balance, and Adams won over Jefferson, seventy-one to sixty-eight.

THE ISSUES of distorting facts, casting doubt on personal character, implying unsavory liaisons, picturing the consequences of misused power, and appealing to those interested in preserving a political group raise questions about how blogging impacts elections. What are the ethics of persuasive techniques? How can readers evaluate the legitimacy of what bloggers write? How do they penetrate the disguise of assumed names and political poses to discover the true motivations of bloggers?

WHAT IF the second President of the United States had been Thomas Jefferson instead of John Adams? What if he had not steered the country through a particularly delicate diplomatic crisis to avoid a second war with a major military power, a war that the United States was not prepared to wage? What if he had not strengthened the military by resurrecting the navy and authorizing a ten-thousand-soldier army? What if he had not helped establish the principle that only the federal government could act as the U.S. representative in international affairs? What if John Adams had not created a precedent for putting the country's best interests before political interests? Would the Federalist faction have survived at the expense of national security, identity, and continuity?

A ROOSTER IN THE HENHOUSE?
BLOGGING THOMAS JEFFERSON

The election of 1800 has been labeled the most contentious and perhaps the most significant in this nation's history, contends David McCullough, author of *John Adams* (2002). President John Adams and Vice President Thomas Jefferson vied for the opportunity to lead the nation as the third President. But more than just the identify of the leader was at stake. Would the Constitution stand against yet another change of the guard? Would the contrast between the political philosophies of public figures and the details of their private lives change the course of their political futures and the nation's future?

CAN HE BE TRUSTED?
IS HE AN ENLIGHTENED DEVIL?
Urban Patriot Blog

Better to have remained a subject of London than become a serf of Paris. We must, under all circumstances, resist the temptation to elect this man, this serpent of the so-called enlightenment. We have before us a cunning sorcerer who enchants with words but serves a master across the ocean. He claims to support equality among men but sees only the land-owner as qualified to participate in politics. He speaks of the yeoman farmer and the virtue of working the land when he does not dirty his own hand. This illusion hides an effort to maintain the dominance of Virginia, creating a national plantation.

COMMENT # 1

Add hypocrite to sorcerer! He is the most duplicitous person I have ever met. To your face, he is warm, charming, and agreeable, always careful to keep the conversation superficial unless one disagrees with his viewpoint. Then his veneer of gentility evaporates, and his attack leaves no quarter and takes no prisoners. His intellectual snobbery is

a coward's tactic. He censures and subdues his audience with a dismissal of low intelligence and little knowledge. He has no courage to defend his writings in open debate.
– *Free Speaker*

COMMENT # 2

This "enlightened man" was nothing but a glorified secretary during the 1775–1776 Continental Congress. Rather he was the great compiler, with no original or unique thought. For his statesmanship, he looks to Europe for his instructions, ever seeking the approval of the self-appointed intellectual elite. If they approve, then he advances the idea, regardless of our citizens' views. – *American Patriot*

COMMENT # 3

We must look at his actions, and not listen to his beautiful words, which seek to seduce us all. We need only ask those on his plantation about his seductive nature—for he truly enjoys all the pleasures of ownership. Virginians seek to advance themselves with pretty pictures of pastoral life, but they neglect to see who bears the true burden of their venture. This rooster seeks to make the rest of our country into a henhouse for himself and his masters. He does not believe that "natural rights" extend to slaves, whom he considers sub-human. The Rooster's private actions should awaken us all! – *Free Speaker*

COMMENT # 4

My Christian Brothers, pay heed. We are faced with far more than a political choice in this election. We face a moral choice: a religious President and God or Jefferson and no God. We must fight against this infidel and the curses he will heap upon our society: murder, robbery, rape, adultery, and incest. The only god he recognizes is the god of the French enlightenment. The salvation of his soul is beyond our reach. He long ago sealed his own fate with the pagan rituals and rites he holds in his Monticello home. We must stand resolute that the fetid blood from these dark rituals does not infect the souls of Christians today and in the future. – *Christian Defender*

COMMENT # 5

During the last election, the Enlightened Man's blindness to all but his party moved him to oppose all who disagreed with him. His dealings and actions were conspiratorial. One wonders what plots and manipulations originate with him. We were unfortunate when this impressionable man was sent to replace the well-established Franklin in France. We regret this act as it has served only to make him a radical revolutionary, and we are the worse for it. – *Wary Citizen*

IN REALITY, in 1800, all the issues that colored the election of 1796 were only more pronounced. The federal government faced test after test as it moved from the war for independence to a functioning world power. In that unsettled environment, urban versus agrarian, standing army versus state militias, a central bank, and a professional bureaucracy to implement the government's business shifted the focus from founding a government to operating one. A different kind of leadership would be needed, and the debate over qualifications, character, and personal beliefs intensified and even turned vicious.

The maneuvering behind the scenes created intrigues that engaged some and horrified others. The election of 1800 was so contentious that many thought the young country would not survive the campaign. Some thought that a civil war might break out before the election. Yet the election ended in a tie between Jefferson and Aaron Burr, with President Adams slightly third. The House of Representatives took thirty-six ballots to break the stalemate. Ultimately, the backroom maneuvers of Jefferson's adversary, Alexander Hamilton, convinced one representative to change his vote and support Jefferson.

Once the final ballot was cast, President John Adams supported Jefferson's victory, establishing the principle of a peaceful transfer of power between political parties. A civil war was averted—for the moment.

THE ISSUES in 1800 for using communication technology to reveal unsavory features of candidates' lives parallel the explosion of blogs today. At that time, newspapers replaced pamphlets as the most easily accessible information distribution, and the hunger for the latest tidbit of scandal or innuendo drowned out concerns about whether there were ground rules about what to disclose. Over two hundred years later, with advanced communication technology, bloggers face the same questions that drive political campaign techniques.

Are writers responsible for checking the validity of a rumor, or is raising the question a sufficient reason to write? What is the role of bloggers in the process of identifying, accessing, and sorting out political candidates? What is the function and responsibility of political campaigners, their staffs, and supporters to identify themselves in the blogosphere? Does the cloak of anonymity serve well the watchdog aspect of blogging or merely enable the elevation of rumor and innuendo to the apparent status of fact?

WHAT IF Thomas Jefferson had not won the 1800 election? What would the country have missed under his leadership? What if John Adams had not conceded amicably? What if Jefferson had not struck a conciliatory note in his inaugural address, striving to bring together the contentious factions and set a precedent that is one of the hallmarks of American democracy and admired the world over?

What if Jefferson had not undertaken the further building of the capital city to establish and reflect the tradition, influence, and power of the United States? What if he had not supported the Supreme Court as the final arbiter of constitutionality, the outlawing of foreign slave trade, and blockading the port of Tripoli when the pasha tried to extort an enormous payment? What if he had not initiated the Louisiana Purchase and the Lewis and Clark Expedition? If bloggers had succeeded in sufficiently tarnishing Jefferson's reputation and preventing him from being President, how might history have been changed?

THE PUPPETEER
BLOGGING ALEXANDER HAMILTON

American politics has long been influenced by political advisors, staff, and behind-the-scenes manipulators. Most do not hold office but exert tremendous impact through their positions as "having the ear" of presidents and elected officials. They often make up the top rung of the government bureaucracy system and have been known to maneuver themselves into positions of greater real power than the officials they serve.

IS HE LOYAL?
DOES HIS AMBITION HAVE NO END?
Adamant Man Blog (President John Adams)

Federalists unite! A malignant danger has been revealed to me—one that threatens our enterprise and future. One in our midst seeks to manipulate this election to secure dominance of a radical element in our faction. The foreigner's dark ambitions will only succeed in destroying the greater purpose, the establishment of a balanced, secure system for our hard-won country. We must support the candidates as chosen by our members in Congress and not substitute the Vice for the President.

COMMENT # 1

Since he came into the confidence and protection of our greatest general, this man has been a master puppeteer. His hand has been in every alleyway and backroom of politics, controlling candidates and officials and bending them to his will. Always longing for military conflict and preferring the sword to the pen, he does not abide negotiation or compromise. He seeks only capitulation and surrender of opponents. This trait only worsened with the loss of the general's steadying hand last year. We must resist placing in office one of his puppets. - *Defender of Justice (John Marshall)*

COMMENT # 2

He is more complex than that picture would portray. His willingness to take on all opponents—political, physical, and philosophical—must remind us of his work to secure acceptance of the Constitution. That he is a patriot, there is no doubt. He had a shining future, which ambition has eroded. We must stem the tide of his great game and save the country. Our liberty would be a price too dear to pay for party loyalty in the face of this malevolent design. – *The Negotiator (John Jay)*

COMMENT # 3

I fear that if he is successful, we will again become subjects of the British Crown. He may deliver us into the hands of that artificial system where men's inheritance and wealth are valued more than their abilities. He readily admits that he seeks to install an aristocracy to rule the people and profit from the work of their hands. This despotism was the reason we threw off British rule. His dark aims must be halted. – *Patriotic Opposer (Aaron Burr)*

COMMENT # 4

Democracy is a noble system but is subject to manipulation by charismatic, talented leaders who would seize the power to become tyrants. Congress and our retired general made him commander of American forces. Now he seeks to prolong the crisis with France, advocating war. He seeks to use this crisis to bring the Federalist Party under his leadership. We must heed the example of Julius Caesar, who consolidated power among a loyal military, expanded his influence in the empire, and returned to the cheers of the Roman people. The Roman Senate could not but proclaim him emperor or risk riot and chaos. We must avoid this pattern at all cost. – *Defender of Justice (John Marshall)*

IN REALITY, during the election of 1800, Alexander Hamilton tried to undermine the candidacy of President John Adams in favor of Thomas Pinckney. He manipulated several Cabinet Secretaries that Adams inherited from George Washington. Realizing that some were not loyal, Adams dismissed the Hamiltonian Secretaries. Hamilton published an anti-Adams pamphlet—a move that apparently worked as Thomas Jefferson and Aaron Burr, the two opposition candidates, won the most votes with Adams in third place.

As Secretary of the Treasury, Hamilton instigated the nation's economic system and devised a system of credit that allowed the new country to function before adequate revenue could be collected. He created a large network of customs officials that Jefferson feared as a bloated bureaucracy designed to bolster Hamilton's power. As a result of the hatred between Burr and Hamilton, based in part on Hamilton's slurs on Burr's integrity, the two fought a duel. Hamilton shot in the air; Burr shot to kill—and succeeded.

THE ISSUES reflected in these imagined blogs raise questions of veracity and visibility. As blogging moves into the mainstream of communication, some bloggers identify themselves and their blogs, but the nature of free speech without acknowledged identity can be seductive. What if all bloggers were forced to add their personal, validated, and verified name to everything written on the Internet? How would the revelation of personal identify change the content, the tone, and the impact of blogs? Is freedom of expression combined with secrecy the real lure of blogging? What does that suggest about the state of democracy?

WHAT IF Alexander Hamilton had been permanently exiled from political influence? What if he had not created the Bank of the United States? What if his economic plan had failed? What if he had succeeded in pressing for war against France under the Adams administration? What if he had failed in advocating for Jefferson over Burr? What if Alexander Hamilton had eventually become President? How might blogs have intensified the antagonism? How did Hamilton's role set the pattern for the many "influencers" to follow?

With each election of a new President of the United States, communication technology has evolved. From Paul Revere's ride through the countryside to herald the coming of the British to the pamphlets privately printed to lambaste an opponent to newspapers printing letters vilifying and supporting candidates, the founding fathers dealt with the issues of information and opinion dissemination just as we do today. The means change; the motives and the messages remain. By the middle of the nineteenth century, the Civil War brought new technologies and further struggles of a developing country that blogging might have influenced.

"A Rail Splitter for President?"

CHAPTER 5

BLOGGING A NATION DIVIDED:
A Rail Splitter for President?

A decade of conflict-riddled compromises over the question of slavery and state's rights had barely preserved the fragile Union. Within its wake, divisions deepened in both political parties. If communication technology had added blogging to the divisive political atmosphere, how would the outcome of the presidency of Abraham Lincoln and the Civil War have been altered?

A PARTY DIVIDED

Many Republicans initially did not embrace Lincoln's nomination. They believed that he was not qualified for the presidency or presentable in public. For his part, Lincoln had extraordinary interpersonal skills that garnered deep and lasting friendships, and he was a masterful political strategist.

PROTECT THE UNION BLOG

We are the laughing stock of an entire nation. The press accounts of our party's convention only prove our folly. They say that the conduct of the Republican Party in the nomination is a remarkable indication of small intellect, growing smaller. They pass over statesmen and able men, and they take up a fourth-rate lecturer who cannot speak good grammar. We are stuck, my friends, in a rotten situation. Either we support this nominee, or we risk losing to a Democrat. We are lost either way!

 COMMENT #1

Look at him—the unlikely fellow seems all legs and arms, with abnormally large hands and feet. To view his face is to look at melancholy itself. I cannot bear it for long, as it affects me deeply, creating a sense of melancholy that threatens to overwhelm me and sweep me away into depression and immobility. Surely if this strange character ascends to the highest office, our nation will suffer the greatest depression of mood ever conceived—impacting not only our national character but also our economy, productivity, and creativity at the same time. We must do whatever necessary to ensure that he does not send his pall over the population. – *Bated and Switched*

 COMMENT #2

Our national mood will not be the only depressed area of our country, for our economy will greatly suffer. Many may not be aware that this Lincoln pushed through the Illinois State Assembly an economic development plan that brought our state into the abyss of a deep depression. His disregard for our state's precarious economic situation and his blind insistence on the measure led to widespread suffering among the Illinois people. His recklessness should caution us all. – *Michigan Man*

 COMMENT #3

You are trying to make a silk purse out of a sow's ear, my friend. I am not certain that it is possible. Still, we cannot be certain that he will not lose. There is much fervor in the country about his oration and appearances, and it is possible that the Democrats could disintegrate under the weight of Douglas' policies. Either we direct this movement or risk it going in a direction that is antithetical to our interests. It seems that we have no choice but to engage in the campaign as Lincoln's surrogates—much as it might be to our distaste. A good show will certainly be rewarded. – ***Weed in the Garden***

COMMENT #4

As for his appeal, gentlemen, let me assure you that it is genuine. I was much impressed with the speech and demeanor of Mr. Lincoln when I saw him at the Cooper Union in New York. Even though he is among the most homely looking men that I ever have seen, a strange and appealing transformation occurs when he speaks. In general, he is dour—indeed, melancholy and even sad—but as he speaks, his face becomes animated. His hands move in the air with a grace and elegance that one would not suspect moments earlier. This Lincoln is indeed impressive, despite his frontier background. I will prevail upon my husband and all those I encounter to support such a statesman. Had I the ability, he would have my vote. – ***Cooper Union Lady***

COMMENT #5

For his part, we must give credit to Lincoln. He played each piece on this chess board with perfection, moving with an invisible hand. He seems to have met and befriended every person in Illinois, and several in New England, Indiana, and the rest of the West. He has turned each obstacle into an asset—whether it is his poor, uneducated frontier upbringing or his loss to Senator Douglas. He utilizes the press and publications to his advantage, building his national reputation at each turn. No matter the venue or place, Lincoln has been there. – ***Weed in the Garden***

COMMENT #6

All Republicans, no matter their former affiliation must unite behind Lincoln and put aside past disagreements, for the future of our party. Should we follow the example of the Democrats and split into several parties, I fear we will disintegrate without chance of repair. Lincoln is our man, and we must all do our utmost to succeed. – *Tribuner*

IN REALITY, on May 17, 1860, Abraham Lincoln won the nomination of the Republican Party. He was a surprise victor at the Republican National Convention. New York Governor William Henry Seward was the favorite, especially with the support of Thurlow Weed, the Republican political boss. However, Lincoln worked through several loyalists to consolidate support in the western states of Illinois, Indiana, Michigan, and Ohio. While Seward led on the first ballot of the Chicago convention, he did not achieve a majority. On the second ballot, he lost ground to Lincoln, who gained a majority on the third ballot. After the bitter debates in the convention, Republicans did not initially embrace Lincoln's nomination.

In the end, Lincoln was able to unify Republican support behind his candidacy by reaching out to his defeated rivals and appealing to their commitment to the party. Seward, the defeated candidate, engaged in a speaking tour on Lincoln's behalf, while Bates and Chase ensured support in their states. Bates also was key in reaching out to the German-American population—an important voting bloc at the time.

THE ISSUES that these blogs represent are still viable. The strong tendency to place personalities before principles, the desire to dwell upon the superficiality of appearances and trivialities instead of on substantive issues, and the force of oppositional politics driving commentary are features of the current blogosphere. Fortunately, characteristics of the "smart mob" are also in play where eventually moderate and judicious opinions emerge.

WHAT IF the power of modern blogging had been able to circumvent the election of Abraham Lincoln? What might have happened if these modern blogging engines with all their power and fury had been available to Lincoln's opponents to ridicule his appearance, make fun of his backwoods roots, and single out any number of Lincoln's awkward moments? Would the country have been deprived of one of its greatest Presidents and the Union been dissolved? In 1860, what if Lincoln had lost the election?

A NATION DIVIDED

The period from May 1860 to November 1860 in American history may be rightly described as one of the most contentious and conflict ridden periods of our long conflicted past. The growing schism of sectionalism divided the nation over slavery, economics, and race. The Band-Aid approaches that had kept the nation together for a decade were coming apart, and the deep divisions that would result in the Civil War were strongly evident in politics.

POPULAR SOVEREIGNTY BLOG

Lincoln must be stopped, or our country will be split in two. Our country stands on the precipice of a decision that may forever change its nature. Our Founding Fathers created a country of the people, by the people, and for the people. They wisely understood that the only way to protect the Union was to allow citizens of each state to decide policy. Whether through lack of education or experience, this Western Man does not comprehend the wisdom of this plan.

COMMENT #1

Should the Illinois rail splitter succeed, the national government will seize our property and destroy our economy. States rights are not the only issue here. We do not speak only of Constitutional interpretation but rights of property and ownership. While well intentioned, Senator Douglas is but a Northerner and cannot appreciate the threat that the Republicans pose to individual liberty. Only a Southerner can defend against the consolidation of our national government and the tyranny it will rain upon our people. – *Kentucky Ridge*

COMMENT #2

A Lincoln presidency would be a disaster! He is a radical abolitionist. Remember the draft resolution he circulated for comment while he served in the House of Representatives. He sought immediate freedom for all slaves everywhere—providing no choice to property owners and allowing for compensation that would never equal the true value of their labor – *First Confederate*

COMMENT #3

My friends, let us not lose sight of the real danger that faces our country. The Republican backwoods candidate threatens the purity of women and the dignity of our race. Should he prevail, he will institute a methodical program of amalgamation and miscegenation that will spell an end to the white race in America. Our wives, daughters, and indeed mothers will not be safe from the lascivious desires of the Negro man. We in the South have had to protect our women from their covetousness nature—what will happen if they are turned loose on the general population? I fear that a regime of rape, seduction, and fornication will ensue, leaving no white woman safe. Protect the virtue of the fair and innocent—defeat this Republican. – *Popular Sovereignty*

COMMENT #4

Not only is he a clumsy political leader, Douglas brings shame and indignity upon our esteemed party! He marches around the country in an unseemly manner advancing his own cause. Does he not have surrogates who are willing to speak for him? This activity belies a deeper problem of organization and delegation. What would he do as

President? Douglas is far more dangerous to this country and our cause than Lincoln. – *Southern Patriot*

COMMENT #5

These Black Republicans must be stopped at every turn—not only in the presidential elections but at all levels of government: national, state, and local. They advance a mythic chimera of freedom for which they have no concrete plan. Should they succeed, the result will be far worse than uncultivated lands. Our economy will collapse, our glorious, refined way of life will disappear, and we will be taxed into poverty in order to support the millions of freemen who will roam our streets with no place to live and no task to undertake. – *Southern Patriot*

COMMENT #6

Fellow Democrats, we must discontinue this internal bickering for the good of our nation, or we will hand the Republicans victory. Our country will become the joke of the world. With this "slang-whanging stump speaker" at our head, our national reputation will decline. He is not presentable in public. Like the frontier cousin who visits New York, his clothes are perpetually wrinkled, ill-fitting, and chronically disheveled. Such a character cannot suddenly change into a properly presentable gentleman representing the dignity of our nation. – *Popular Sovereignty*

COMMENT #7

You are correct, Popular Sovereignty. Get out of the race. Show that you are a real man. Give Breckinridge the opportunity to win for the Democrats. You should just admit that you truly are Lincoln's partner in abolishing slavery. You have conspired to give him a national reputation and are every bit his partner as was Herndon, that notorious radical abolitionist. Not satisfied with managing Lincoln's Senate

> campaign, today he agitates against slavery—which cannot
> be without Lincoln's blessing. Douglas defied his President
> to oppose slavery in Kansas despite its popular support.
> – *Southern Patriot*

IN REALITY, popular sovereignty, or letting the states and territories decide the issues most important to a region, appealed to America's sense of local self government. It dominated the election debate and the position of Democrat Stephen Douglas of Illinois. The Republic was nearly destroyed by trying to let the principle of popular sovereignty decide the question of slavery.

Democratic Senator Stephen A. Douglas of Illinois championed the notion that a state's populace should decide whether it wanted to be a free or slave state. His "Popular Sovereignty" doctrine was his campaign platform during his senatorial and presidential bids. However, Douglas broke with Democratic President James Buchanan, who supported a pro-slavery draft of the Kansas state constitution. This opposition to Kansas being a slave state gained Douglas the enmity of the South. In 1860, when he was chosen as the Democratic nominee for president, Southern delegates held their own convention in Cincinnati and nominated John Breckinridge of Kentucky. Joshua Bell was nominated by the Constitutional Union party, which sought to take the issue of slavery out of the election by ignoring it.

The split within the Democratic party was so deep that Breckinridge did not campaign in the North, advancing his pro-slavery and states rights platform only in slave states. The Democratic Party was split into so many factions with each garnering votes that Lincoln barely obtained 40 percent of the popular vote which was enough to win the election. It was truly a house divided.

THE ISSUES reflected in these blogs reveal one of the darkest sides of blogger and blogging behavior in that a number of individuals are always "trolling" the community ready to post controversial messages that attempt to elicit an emotional response. If mean inflammatory remarks are exchanged, frequently there results a quick race to the bottom of the barrel in terms of civility and decorum. Under these conditions, freedom of speech and a genuine discussion of ideas get lost in the heat of the moment.

WHAT IF in 1860, the Democrats had settled on a single candidate and not become a completely fractured party? Would the Democratic Party have won the election? Would the Civil War have been averted or postponed? Would slavery have been continued in the South and extended into the territories?

UNITED WE STAND, DIVIDED WE FALL?

In his House Divided Speech, Abraham Lincoln said, "I believe this government cannot endure, permanently half slave and half free. I do not expect the house to fall—but I do expect it will cease to be divided. It will become all one thing or all the other." Short of one side surrendering its beliefs, the only way for this to be achieved was war or attrition. While Lincoln hoped for attrition, reality gave him war.

LIBERATOR BLOG

Let not the current political debate blind us to the realities of Lincoln's stance on slavery. He pretends to stand for morality on this issue, wherein he would continue to protect and support this abhorrent institution in our Southern states. It is a wonder that the Democrats do not understand his ruse. Slavery must be abolished in all places for all time—not only in our new territories. The greatest irony is that Lincoln's great popularity due to his "House Divided" speech belies his true intent. He is interested in Union over morality and would prefer to preside over a wholly slave country over a half-free nation.

COMMENT #1

How can Lincoln unite the country when he cannot even unite his own house? Springfield is rife with stories of Mary's hysteria and abuse of her much taller husband, with scenes of him ushering the children out of the house while her blows rain down upon him. Perhaps he should heed his own advice and attend to his own domestic affairs. – *Bitter Pill*

COMMENT #2:

This Lincoln that the Democrats portray as being radically opposed to slavery is no such person. I remember well his undistinguished congressional career and his proposition for our capital district. True, he sought to make Washington a slave-free area, but the deceit with which he did so demonstrated his duplicity. His proposal also included a provision that required the authorities to deliver up to their owners all fugitive slaves escaping into this District. He is no abolitionist. He is a slave hound from Illinois.

– *Freedom for All*

COMMENT #3

Better to have an honest supporter of slavery than a tepid compromiser! America today stands on the edge of a knife, one that will cut us to shreds. Indecision is our enemy, as is the threat of secession or the continuance of our immoral and reprehensible evil. Each day that we assent to slavery, we are complicit in it. We point to the Faustian bargain that our Founding Fathers made in order to achieve independence, but they sold the moral soul of this country in the process. We need a President who will be fully on the side of Right, fully abolishing slavery. No more compromise.

– *The Liberator*

COMMENT #4

A higher law regulates our authority and devotes it to noble purposes. The territory is a part of the common heritage of mankind, bestowed by the Creator of the universe. We are stewards. We must guide it toward the principles of

Christianity and God's law, or seek eternal damnation. This law defies the chains of slavery. – *Primary Candidate*

COMMENT #5

Enough talk and enough politics! We must follow the righteous action of John Brown, that venerable martyr, who knew the only path toward abolishing slavery. Neither Southern plantation owners nor their Northern conspirators will free the slaves until they are forced to do so. Indeed, when the governments use military troops to enforce the unjust Fugitive Slave Law, we are left no choice. We must take to arms in order to free these innocents. – *The Stationmaster*

IN REALITY, the 1860 election was the culmination of a clash between northern and southern states concerning the issues of slavery and states rights. The seeds of this conflict can be detected in the earliest days of the United States, rooted in the meaning of the Constitution. Throughout the nineteenth century, government officials sought to avoid a conflagration by employing a variety of compromises. Although they achieved their short-term objectives, these maneuvers added to the grievances of both sides. In the end, political leaders were able to delay an open fight, but they did not address the underlying disagreements themselves.

In the decade prior to Lincoln's presidential run, the famous Compromise of 1850 sought to keep the Union together. The legislation included the following provisions: admitting California to the Union as a free state, prohibiting the slave trade in Washington, D.C., allowing slavery to continue, and ruling that northern states were obligated to return fugitive slaves to their former owners in the Fugitive Slave Act.

These basic differences were exacerbated by the issue of slavery. As the country expanded, the question of slavery became more and more of an irritant. As each state sought entry into the Union, the question of parity between slave and free states became sharper, with the South seeking to protect the numbers of Senators and Representatives from slave states, while the North attempted to allow slavery to "die a natural death."

William Lloyd Garrison was one of the voices against slavery. For thirty-five years, he published *The Liberator*. He advocated the doctrine of "immediacy" and was the leading voice in the movement. He also created anti-slavery societies in the North through which non-violent, immediate emancipation would be achieved. Garrison viewed the U.S. Constitution to be a document that protected slavery; therefore, he considered it to be void

THE ISSUES revealed in these blogs reflect the development of faster communication technology. Abraham Lincoln took maximum advantage of the telegraph to build his presence on the national political scene much like political candidates in the 2004 election used blogging effectively for the first time. He understood how the telegraph was utilized by the press to give next-day coverage to events around the country. This advance sped up the news cycle and knit together remote parts of the country. A senatorial candidate speaking in Ottawa, Illinois, could impact the political debate in Boston, St. Louis, Charleston, New York, Washington, or San Francisco. Because of the telegraph, Lincoln positioned himself on the greater national stage.

WHAT IF a statesman of lesser discernment and vision had had to deal with the issue of slavery facing the nation? Would we have maintained a Union? Would slaves have been emancipated? Would the southern states have been allowed to form a new country? Was the Civil War inevitable? Why did the resolution of slavery, evident as a conflict, during the founding of the country, simmer for so long? If bloggers had been around, would it likely have happened sooner rather than later?

Lincoln set the stage for using whatever practical means were at hand to spread his message, but he could not have foreseen how the evolution of that technology would impact the presidencies of Franklin Roosevelt, John Kennedy, and Lyndon Johnson. How blogging would have altered their experiences almost two hundred years after George Washington rode through the streets pulled by six white horses reveals the rapid development of new means for expressing the voice of the people.

"Daddy's Little President"

| CHAPTER 6 |

BLOGGING TWENTIETH CENTURY PRESIDENTS
AN AMERICAN HITLER, A DADDY'S BOY, AND A CROOKED TEXAN?

BLOGGER'S CODE: DO NOT USE THE BLOG TO WILLFULLY CAUSE HARM.

Historians credit President George Washington with establishing dignity and respect for the office of the Presidency due to his deportment and actions. Many of Washington's successors have been accused of over-reaching, of expanding the power of the Presidency beyond its Constitutional boundaries, and of using the office to advance their own policy vision at the party's expense.

DICTATOR AND SOCIALIST?
BLOGGING FRANKLIN ROOSEVELT

President Franklin Roosevelt, who extended the powers of the Presidency as much as any President, held power in times of great crisis and great technological change. With the Great Depression, he faced the worst crisis in the country since the Civil War. He had supreme confidence in his ability to communicate with ordinary Americans, and he had a new technology to use for his political purposes, the radio. He had a stable of good speech writers, a sense of pace and rhythm in his speeches, and ability when he spoke on radio to convince listeners he was talking directly to them. He instituted a series of radio "fireside chats" to explain to the American people what he was doing to solve the nation's problems. These fireside chats were one of the most effective one-way conversations ever employed with the American people.

Bloggers would have rushed to comment when Roosevelt contemplated a third term in office, something no President had ever done.

CAN WE BEAR THIS FOR A THIRD TERM?
Cactus Jack Blog

Enough is enough. For the past eight years, I put my party ahead of my principles and bloodied my knuckles to put a stop to our national nightmare. No longer can I play the junior partner while headquarters engages in creeping despotism. We have enough dictators in this world—we do not need one in the United States.

COMMENT #1

We should have known what was coming during the 1934 Convention, when his minions maneuvered to change the party rules. We followed blindly as he spit in the face of the party founders to overturn the two-thirds rule and grab the power of nominating the vice presidential candidate from the delegates. This repression foreshadowed his actions.
- *Mr. Democrat*

COMMENT #2

Let us take heed of the German example, when a little known man used democracy to ascend to power—first through tiny steps that were cheered as necessary in order to pull the country out of its economic ruin. Only late in the day did some realize that this Little Colonel had seized absolute power. So far we have been able to repel those moves here, but we may not be so successful in a third term. No, we must stop his march toward dictatorship now.
- *Mr. Sam*

COMMENT #3

He plays coy as his New Dealers ride herd to secure his re-nomination. His arrogance is exceeded only by his

ambition. Two terms are not enough for him, as they were for Washington and Jefferson. He pledged an oath with me that he would not seek a third term. I should have known that a faithless man is the same to everyone, not just his wife.
– *Cactus Jack*

COMMENT #4

Our beloved First Lady is very much like America. Her husband's infidelity is not limited to their marriage bed. Just as he keeps several extras on hand at the White House, so he prefers socialism and militarism to democracy. He dances with the labor unions instead of business and plays the savior to London at the expense of America's youth. He is clever enough to hide his intent. The only question is whether we can generate enough support for another Democrat before he locks up the nomination. – *Mr. Democrat*

COMMENT #5

We will need an honorable man to challenge the President directly. We will have to smoke out the President into the open and reveal his plan. We will have to demonstrate mismanagement and evil intent from the beginning by him and his New Dealers. We shall make them out to be a gang of blackguards. Since you have compared the vice presidency to a spare tire on an automobile, we can use that as a way to explain that you were kept out of the loop about the real intent but roped in to do the President's bidding. – *Mr. Sam*

IN REALITY this blog and comments represent ideas circulating during the 1940 election prior to the Democratic National Convention in Chicago. They show the Democratic opposition to President Roosevelt seeking a third term. In 1932 and 1936, Vice President John Nance Garner, described by *Time* as "a tough little Texan who is built like a fire hydrant," was FDR's running mate and served as Vice President during the first two terms.

Franklin Delano Roosevelt is considered one of America's greatest Presidents. In 1932, he was elected to rescue the country from the Great Depression. In 1929, the American economy began its downward spiral with a recession that began in August and the stock market crash in October. In addition to economic collapse, the national outlook also was negative. One quarter of America's workforce was unemployed, with no prospect of a turnaround. In 1932, by the time of the election, every sector of the economy had contracted, 10,000 banks had failed, 13 million people had lost their jobs, and capital investment had declined from $16 billion to $300 million.

Franklin Delano Roosevelt offered the American people two things that they desperately needed: leadership and hope. By 1940, Roosevelt's accumulation of power had begun to worry many of his critics and this imaginary blog reflects the feelings of his opponents.

THE ISSUES in this blog and comments illustrate favorite tactics of political bloggers everywhere. They feel free to go to any length to attack the opposing side to block their next political move. If your opponent is powerful and ambitious, inevitably the extreme opposition compares you to Adolf Hitler. In political blogging, a working principle is to demonize the opposition in the strongest terms with slight regard to the facts or the truth. Forgetting the facts and just concentrating on being heard has always characterized the most extreme and least responsible expressions of free speech, especially in politics.

WHAT IF in 1940, the opposition members of his party had succeeded in defeating Franklin Roosevelt's attempt at a third term of office? Would the new President have led us into World War II? Would the Japanese have attacked Pearl Harbor? Would the country finally have come out of the Great Depression? Would the New Deal have been replaced with some other "deal"?

ARE WE MOVING TOWARD SOCIALISM?
Free Enterprise Advocate Blog

Our nation is at risk from two directions simultaneously. Economically, the current administration has pursued a policy of deficit spending that threatens future generations, while implementing a series of measures that threaten our free enterprise system. Large, wasteful bureaucracies now force the government to borrow and tax in record amounts. As for our defense, the Administration has cut military budgets in order to feed its large government agencies. As war rages in Europe and freedom loving countries are swallowed whole by the German monster, we lie exposed and unprepared—a tempting target for Hitler.

COMMENT #1

Roosevelt has marched this country toward war from the beginning. His plan all along has been to support the war effort of Britain and France. Should they not succeed, he will take us to war—with or without congressional approval. In the meantime, Roosevelt will use the war as an excuse to impose socialism on this country. He will ally himself with Stalin, as well as Churchill, and import the Soviet system. We must warn the American people that his talk of war is a deception for a far more dangerous plan—to destroy the American system. – *Mr. Republican*

COMMENT #2

He is in bed with the labor unions and their red supporters. His New Deal was the first step in promoting the interests of socialism against the interests of business and capital. As we saw during the Flint Sit-Down Strike, he will side with labor's goal of expropriating private property for the benefit of the working class. Selective service is the next step, making all men equal, regardless of class, creed, race, or position to fulfill the socialist vision. – *The Gangbuster*

COMMENT #3

The President is no friend of labor. True, he has created many bureaus to address the emergency situation caused by the Depression, but he is not one of us. His patrician airs will forever separate him from our cause. The danger is that he would willingly send millions of workers to their deaths. The President says he hates war and will work for peace, but his acts do not match his words. He has schemed for years to involve us in war. – *Leading Labor*

COMMENT #4

WPA, NRC, TVA—what are these in reality? With each new letter combination that the Administration proposes, the citizens of this country grow less and less free. We continue to see the accumulation of power in Washington at the expense of state home-rule and individual independence. Congress has surrendered to alphabetical commissars who deeply believe the American people need to be regimented by powerful overlords in order to be saved. If not for the opposition, this country would be doomed. – *Defender of Democracy*

COMMENT #5

We must elect an honest man of the people who has worked with his hands and known hunger. We must elect Wendell Willkie. Otherwise, we yield to the appetite for power and the vaunting ambitions of a man who plays with the lives of human beings for a pastime. I think the reelection of the President for a third term would be a national evil of the first magnitude. – *Leading Labor*

IN REALITY Roosevelt could not please his critics. Republicans and Conservative Democrats accused him of being too close to labor and incrementally moving the country toward socialism. A major union leader, however, charged FDR with turning to the right and reversing his pro-labor policies. Nevertheless, these strange bedfellows agreed on one thing—they saw Roosevelt as marching the country toward war.

THE ISSUES in the world of blogging reveal that all sides seem to be willing to go to any length to play upon fear or the baser human emotions to get their negative points of view across on the issues. The opposition's values are cast as "evils," and their positions exaggerated and smeared, their policies simplified and attacked.

WHAT IF Roosevelt had lost the 1940 election and Wendell Willkie had become President? Would the policies of the New Deal have been reversed? Would free enterprise according to the Republican tradition have been reinstituted? Would Willkie have led the nation to war?

HOW DID WE GET TO CAMELOT?
BLOGGING JOHN F. KENNEDY

Every so often a new face emerges in American politics, bringing with him a fresh confidence, a change in pace, and the perspective of a younger generation. This candidate becomes the symbol of the hopes and dreams of his generation and the greater American public. He galvanizes new voters while pleasing the party establishment. His youth trumps his inexperience, and his candidacy captures the imagination of the electorate.

Often, this rising political star utilizes new communications technology for his campaign, creating a new dynamic in American politics. When novelty and technology combine with a message to create a popular image of a candidate, the results can be unexpected.

President Lincoln knew how to use the telegraph-newspaper combination to broadcast his message widely around the country. President William McKinley changed the rules of the front porch speech by bringing in crowds of people by rail. President Franklin Delano Roosevelt used radio to establish a personal relationship with voters. After World War II, the new invention of television waited to be leveraged for political campaigns. Television seemed to be waiting for President John F. Kennedy, both in life and in death, but first he had to face the issue of his Roman Catholic religion.

WOULD THE PRESIDENT REPORT TO THE POPE?
Religious Watchdog Blog

Every Catholic is necessarily part of the Pope's extended army. Each Catholic marches through life with the knowledge that at any time he may be called upon by the Pope to carry out some mission in the name of the Church. What will happen if we allow one of the Pope's army to have control over our government? For our country's future, we must not fall into this temptation.

COMMENT #1

The young prince is not so far removed from the Pope. His father was close to the Pope as cardinal, and the whole family attended the Papal investiture. With those personal ties, the danger is clear. – *Citizen for Religious Freedom*

COMMENT #2

We all know that each Catholic takes an oath of fealty to the Pope through the Knights of Columbus. I read it in my church's newsletter that Catholics promise to wage relentless war, secretly and openly, against all heretics, Protestants, and Masons. They are directed to extirpate them from the face of the whole earth. Now, tell me, who is going to do the "directing" except the Pope or his corrupt Bishops and Cardinals? And, who are they going to wage relentless war against? The Soviets? No. Castro? No. Communists? No. They're going to wage war against Americans. – *True American*

COMMENT #3

Yeah, my Dad told me about that. He said that in 1928 he heard it when Al Smith ran for President. He said that it was even in the official government Congressional Record. I don't know, but if it was in your church newsletter, then it must be true. Christians wouldn't lie about such a thing, and neither would the government. Our pastor hasn't said anything about it yet, but I'm sure he will. Anyway, why was this country created if not to protect Christianity from the Catholics? – *Son of the Revolution*

COMMENT #4

This young Boston Altar Boy already has proven himself to be a tool of the Catholic Church. I remember when I invited him to speak at a building fund dinner in Philadelphia. The whole event raised money for an interfaith chapel in the Grace Baptist Temple to be dedicated to the memory of the four Army chaplains killed in 1943 on the *Dorchester*. Who better to speak than a Catholic Congressman, a veteran himself, who lost a brother in the War? At virtually the last minute, the Altar Boy calls me and says that the Archdiocese of Philadelphia isn't comfortable with him speaking about *interfaith* issues. Not only did he back out of the appearance, but he really put us in a bind. If he becomes President, every Catholic priest, bishop, and cardinal will control him—not to mention the Pope! – *Philadelphia Preacher*

COMMENT #5

Our American culture is at stake. I don't say it won't survive, but it won't be what it was. With an Altar Boy at the helm, we will see Church doctrine implemented in policy initiatives. We will see favorable treatment to other Catholics. I wouldn't be surprised if the Pope had his own White House bedroom! I have heard from thousands of my readers and listeners who are just plain scared of the impending Catholic regime. We must do everything possible to prevent that from happening. – *Guidepost*

IN REALITY Kennedy's Catholicism was a major issue in the 1960 campaign. Anti-Catholic sentiment was not new to America or its political scene. Protestant immigrants to the New World sought refuge from the dominance of established religion. Even if the established religion was Protestant in nature—Anglican or Lutheran—minority groups such as the Pilgrims, Quakers, Shakers, Mennonites, Methodists, and others were persecuted as the Catholic Church had persecuted other sects in the pre-Reformation era.

Democratic Party leaders were skeptical about a Catholic candidate, and they did not embrace Kennedy until after he had proven that he could overcome this prejudice in the electorate. Kennedy's campaign team made the primary in Wisconsin its first test. While Kennedy won, when the results were analyzed, he was put over the top by his wins in primarily Catholic districts.

THE ISSUES of how religious controversy can stir up the blogs are with us still. Blogs continue to make use of the unverified anecdote, the strongest exaggerations, and the outright smear to denigrate an opponent. Making the Office of the President the complete captive of the Papacy would have been a favorite if blogging technology had been available for the 1960 general election. Since blogs are vehicles for spreading propaganda, frequently a few incidents, taken out of context, serve the argument of the blogger. This is a common practice in creating propaganda, especially when it is designed to play upon fear and prejudice.

WHAT IF the tactics of the anti-Catholic faction of Kennedy's opponents had succeeded in denying him the nomination? What if a person's religion had become the single most important issue in an election? What message would this send to other religious minorities?

DADDY'S LITTLE PRESIDENT?
Freedom's Watchdog Blog

In 1954, the Young Princeling dodged the McCarthy issue. The best you can say is that he was indisposed due to his back surgery. We know that his brother—today his campaign manager—actively worked for Joe McCarthy digging up dirt with which to crucify people in his hearings. More to the point, Papa was an active supporter of McCarthy during his heyday. The Kid never gave an unequivocal repudiation of the family's support of this witch-hunter, just self-serving excuses.

COMMENT #1

Unfortunately, the Father's influence on the son is profound. The Kid is just a marionette at the end of strings that his father pulls. The kid brother—now that's another story. He's Papa's street fighter—every bit as willing to get his hands dirty as dear old Dad. Given Dad's affinity toward McCarthy and Dad's history supporting Hitler, one wonders how the Kid's foreign policy would be shaped. No, we face too many dangers to have men like these in power. – *Rightful Candidate*

COMMENT #2

Everyone's talking about how the Pope will be in charge of the country should the Kid win. Well, it's not the Pope I'm afraid of; it's the pop. A vote for the son is a vote for the father. – *Number 33*

COMMENT #3

The Kid is too young and inexperienced for this job. Look at his record. In the House, he got swept up by the prevailing winds of anti-Communism. The means justified the ends, if it was popular. No, he's too ambitious and even a little foolish, a young man too quick to grasp at the grand prize. He doesn't have the backbone to stand his ground and fight for a moral issue if it is not popular. – *Rightful Candidate*

COMMENT #4

He's gotta be the luckiest son-of-a-bitch alive. How many men in the War exhibited heroism every day? How many saved buddies? How many overcame tremendous physical challenges? Yet this young buck gets all the glory. And, how was he portrayed? As the Father's Son. The press only needed a Holy Ghost to make the picture complete.
– *Master of the Senate*

COMMENT #5

That's the way it's gone his whole career. He wouldn't have been in the Navy if not for Daddy's interference. I've seen the file—he doesn't qualify medically. When the Navy docs got a look at his insides, they shipped him right home. The Kid's been sickly all his life—have you seen the pictures of him? And, he has serious back problems—SERIOUS. Remember the pictures of him being helicoptered home after a back operation? I say he's not fit for the rig-ahs of office. – *Number 33*

IN REALITY Kennedy's father, Joseph P. Kennedy, had cultivated his son to fulfill his own ambition of having a Kennedy President. As the son of Irish Catholic immigrants living in Boston, Joseph Kennedy longed to be accepted by Boston's upper class society. He wanted to out-earn, out-influence, and out-succeed them on every level. This vision included the dream of making one of his sons the first Catholic President of the United States.

Ambassador Joseph P. Kennedy groomed his eldest, Joseph Jr., for political office. However, when Joe died in World War II, this ambition was transferred to the oldest surviving son, John Fitzgerald Kennedy. JFK, or "Jack," as he was known, had been a sickly child—contracting the childhood diseases of scarlet fever, diphtheria, and measles—as well as having chronic acute colitis, which began in his 20s.

JFK declared his candidacy for President on January 2, 1960. His main rival was Minnesota Senator Hubert H. Humphrey II, from the liberal wing of the party. The two battled in Wisconsin and West Virginia, with Kennedy eventually prevailing.

THE ISSUES of this blog and comments involve relying on facts not in evidence and guilt by association. They focus on charges of no experience and piggybacking upon another's ambition and money. Using the tactic of innuendo to ridicule, the blogs distort the truth at many levels. Without any proof, the blogs range far and wide based on rumor.

WHAT IF in 1960, these tactics had worked and successfully blocked Kennedy from becoming President? What would have happened if Hubert Humphrey had become President? What would have happened if Richard Nixon had won? How would the Cold War have been fought? Would the Bay of Pigs mission have occurred?

NEGATIVE TELEVISION ADS, THE VIETNAM WAR
BLOGGING LYNDON JOHNSON

Lyndon Johnson's 1964 election campaign was the first to run negative attack television ads, capitalizing on the progress in communication technology. The most famous one—and one that had a profound impact—was called the "Daisy" ad. It featured a little girl in a field of flowers picking the petals and counting: one, two, three, four, five, six, seven, eight, nine, ten. A male voice came on the air with a 10-1 countdown, and the picture faded to film of a mushroom cloud, a universal symbol of a nuclear bomb. Johnson's voice said, "These are the stakes—to make a world in which all of God's children can live, or to go into the dark." Johnson's opponent, Barry Goldwater of Arizona, was only one of his critics whose supporters might have taken advantage of blogs if they had been available.

 ### MR. CONSERVATIVE BLOG

Americans are in danger from the current occupant of the Presidency. Not only does he head the most corrupt, power-mad administration in our country's history, but he also has failed to provide moral leadership or control crime and disorder. On a personal level, this occupant is the phoniest individual that ever came around—manipulating people to achieve his own goals. His domestic programs reflect a slow takeover of the American economy by government "for our own good" while he pursues a liberal social agenda. His creeping Communism chips away at the basis upon which America was created—freedom, liberty, and democracy.

Giving him a mandate in this election will empower him to commit greater evils on the American people.

COMMENT #1

Immorality, moral decay, crime, vice, pornography, race riots in Harlem, New York—the newspapers are filled with these problems on a daily basis thanks to the Democratic Administration under Johnson. Not only are we in a battle with the Soviets, but we are also in a battle here at home—a battle for the very soul of our country. America has only one choice—return to morality or sink deeper into the cesspool of Johnson's filth. – *White Knight*

COMMENT #2

Down here in Texas, we know about Johnson's crimes, and now the world knows. There's corruption, graft, and murder. Billy Sol Estes created a scam with fake cotton crops, for which he received $21 million from the government. When a Federal Agent investigated and discovered how in 1961 Estes stole from the federal government, Estes called his buddy in DC, the Veep. The agent—a Mr. Marshall—wound up with five rifle bullets in his head—a "suicide." Now tell me how a guy can shoot himself with a rifle—let alone five times! – *Texas Ranger*

COMMENT #3

This goes all the way to the top. Johnson's quest is for power. He will stop at nothing to get it. Once Hoover told Kennedy about the Marshall murder, JFK took a personal interest in it. Like the others who could threaten LBJ's future, Kennedy was dead within months. The Texas oil mafia didn't like Kennedy anyway since he was about to eliminate the oil depletion allowance and cost them $100 million in free government subsidies. – *Choice Producer*

COMMENT #4

And, Johnson gets a pass. It doesn't matter how many women he's bedding at the same time—Lady Bird is truly a saint! Or how drunk he is when he's coming off the plane for a campaign stop. Or whether he makes sense in interviews or speeches he gives. So much for journalistic ethics and neutrality. We're back to the days of yellow journalism in the nineteenth century. Trouble is, we don't have our own set of publications to counter their propaganda. – *White Knight*

COMMENT #5

It's the Johnson way. Look at what he did in Austin—bought up all the media outlets, radio, television, and even cable. I've heard that he's either intimidated or purchased newspaper reporters. One thing Johnson doesn't believe in is the First Amendment. No freedom of the press. No freedom of speech. The Johnson way. – *Speechwriter*

IN REALITY although leading by huge margins in every poll, Johnson insisted on running a full-scale campaign, as if he had to earn the vote. His campaign was extraordinarily aggressive, portraying Goldwater as a danger. He leveraged Goldwater's pronouncements on using a nuclear weapon in Vietnam and his vote against the Civil Rights Bill of 1964 to enhance fear within the American electorate. Goldwater's campaign slogan was "In your heart, you know he's right." The Johnson campaign spun it as "In your guts, you know he's nuts." That basically encapsulates the tenor of the campaign.

THE ISSUES for the blogosphere were ripe for an intensely partisan blogging effort. Rumors of immorality, crime, and even murder, as seems to be the custom in many parts of the blogging world, were tossed about seriously, even casually, without proof. Corruption, graft, immoral sex, and implications in murder were the charges most frequently aimed at LBJ, but none seemed to have the power to catch fire.

WHAT IF bloggers and the media had brought to light some of LBJ's more unsavory political activities in Texas? What if LBJ's past had politically caught up with him? What if LBJ had lost the 1964 election to Barry Goldwater? What would have happened to the Civil Rights Movement? Would Barry Goldwater really have used a nuclear bomb in Vietnam?

THE UNDECLARED WAR: VIETNAM
Johnson Lied, Men Died Blog

Did you read about the "second attack" in the Gulf of Tonkin in the paper? Well, my brother is in that division, and he e-mailed me that there were some weird happenings last night—radar problems and a spooky "drill" for a torpedo attack. He never mentioned an actual attack, even though he did two days beforehand. This whole thing about a second attack is a lie!

COMMENT #1

LBJ lied about the Gulf of Tonkin in order to find a premise for the U.S. engaging the Viet Cong. Why would he do this? To trump his political rival Goldwater. There was no attack. There were radar problems. Nothing was hit. Four more years of LBJ and we'll have tens of thousands of dead American soldiers—all for his personal political gain.
- *Expose the Manipulation*

COMMENT #2:

We are provoking attacks, putting our men in harm's way. The Cuban Missile Crisis was one thing—this is another. We have no business being in Vietnam. Our presence there is the cause of the war. If we weren't there, there'd be no fighting. - *Johnson Lied, Men Died*

COMMENT #3

The Viet Cong only wanted to lift the yolk of colonialism, with all of its ills. There was no reason for the French to be there, and we have taken France's place. Kennedy was wrong to send in our "advisors." He has made us into the colonialists in order to expand the American Empire. This is not what the Founding Fathers envisioned. – ***Stop the Oppression***

COMMENT #4

Leave Vietnam now! That is the only choice. Neither candidate believes this, so we must make them accept this point. We must pressure Congress, hold demonstrations, write letters to the editor, expose the cover-up, file charges, sue on behalf of the soldiers, and do whatever we need to do to get our message across. – ***Power to the People***

COMMENT #5

This should be the call to action: sign the petition, contact your Members of Congress, and take to the streets—make your voice heard around the country. Congress will get the message. – ***Power to the People***

IN REALITY when Johnson became President after Kennedy's assassination, he pledged to continue with his predecessor's policies. Approving national security memoranda and plans for covert operations, Johnson began slowly to escalate American involvement in Vietnam. In early 1964, he transferred responsibility for operations in Vietnam from the CIA to the Pentagon. In response to the Gulf of Tonkin resolution passed by Congress to protect the armed forces, Johnson understood that he had the "functional equivalent" of a declaration of war.

THE ISSUES suggested by this blog and these comments cut to the heart and power of blogging itself in the present. The Internet can be leveraged for the advancement of advocacy agendas promoted by a few people. A few highly motivated, technology savvy, well-funded people can come together with a message and use the Internet, e-mail, Web sites, video, and paid advertising to impact public opinion on policy or legislation. The blog also highlights how an online advocacy campaign can recruit grassroots activists to take action in the non-virtual world.

Those with computer know-how can create an e-mail alert in about thirty minutes. A video can be created in a matter of hours, as can a simple Web site. Publishing these items is very quick. All of this can "go live" overnight. With the right message, network, and timing an online advocacy campaign can spread the word, attract supporters, and create action within twenty-four hours. Such is the nature of the modern blogosphere.

WHAT IF the Internet had existed during the 1964 election? Would the Internet have allowed its users to review journalistic standards of the time, like the Drudge Report did regarding *Newsweek's* decision to kill the initial story about President Clinton and Monica Lewinsky? Could bloggers and the Internet have influenced the media to take a different approach to the Gulf of Tonkin Resolution? Could the Internet have mobilized public opinion to prevent a massive widening of the war? Could the Vietnam War have been prevented?

WIDENING THE GREAT PUBLIC CONVERSATION

This retrospective look at elections and some of our more famous Presidents reveals that the impulse to blog or at least to participate in blog-like behavior has been a part of American life since the early republic. Sentiments once contained in pamphlets and editorial pages of newspapers advanced to telegraph, radio, television, and finally the Internet—all the while increasing speed, force, and impact.

Washington, Adams, Jefferson, and their opponents used the printing press to initiate the great conversations of the day, and the discourse could be as harsh, unprincipled, and nasty as the bottom feeders of any modern-day blogging conversation.

Lincoln took advantage of the newest technology, the telegraph, to send electrified messages to newspapers across the country to achieve maximum effect. Thus, the public conversation was extended in geographical coverage and reduced closer to real time.

In the twentieth century, the technology became advanced enough to conduct a one-way conversation in real time through the medium of radio which Franklin Roosevelt mastered through his fireside chats. With the advent of television, the news went live for the American people, and they could fully participate in much of it in real time. John Kennedy was a politician instantly comfortable with the new medium of television and used it with great skill. Lyndon Johnson would mobilize the medium for attack in election ads.

What was missing in all these technologies was a medium for the public itself to engage political figures in great conversations. Not until the Internet and blogs could these public conversations take place—dialogues in almost real time between politicians, their friends, their opponents, interested parties—on a global scale. We can only imagine how American history would have developed had such a technology existed throughout our history.

| PART 3 |

BLOGGING IN THE MYSPACE ERA

"Blogging is a good thing!"

CHAPTER 7

MARTHA HITS A BLOG HOME RUN PETE STRIKES OUT

Celebrities who fall from grace in scandal are not new on the American landscape. Neither are celebrities who fall from grace and redeem themselves rebuilding their lives and careers. What is new about this process is that the attempt to rebuild and reconcile now takes place in the media populated by a world of millions of blogs. In negotiating this treacherous path, some are successful and some fail. Two cases of celebrities who have embarked upon the rebuilding process illustrate the opportunities and pitfalls in cyberspace. One hit a home run, and the other struck out.

MARTHA STEWART SAVES A BRAND

In April 2006, a blogger named Max Stirner, known as Brewrunner to the blogging world, was still thinking about the Martha Stewart's conviction for lying about stock transactions with the ImClone Company. This blogger had been given the assignment in his business law class to analyze business ethics as related to the Martha Stewart case.

Over a year earlier, he had read "Why Martha Stewart Should Go to Heaven and the SEC Should Go to Hell," an article from *Reason Magazine.* He was afraid that the title of the article alone might get him an "F" on the assignment, but he decided to post an entry on his blog, "Against the State," the Blogosphere of the Libertarian Left.

He chose to use the assignment as an opportunity "to argue that the government was the guiltiest party of ethics violations" in prosecuting Stewart for allegedly lying about the reasons she dumped her stock in ImClone. "In the government's never ending quest to punish people for crimes in which there is no victim, it created hundreds if not thousands of victims by calling out the dogs on Martha." Stockholders of Martha Stewart Living Omnimedia and K-Mart lost large percentages of their investments when those stocks tumbled after the prosecution and conviction. On April 13, 2006, at 11:49 p.m., Stirner posted his item with the question, "Which action was the greater evil?"

Where Brewrunner stands on the Martha Stewart issues is not difficult to discern. In the blog, he states his passion for life, laissez-faire, private property rights, and individual liberty. He enumerates a long list of favorite books that includes *Atlas Shrugged*, *The Fountainhead*, and *How I Found Freedom in an Unfree World*. All of these titles are compatible with a libertarian blog.

Brewrunner represented bloggers who lined up in Martha Stewart's behalf when her troubles with the government surfaced. Blogs generally do not take to the middle of the road. That is not their nature. They take strong positions either on the extreme left or extreme right, love 'em or hate 'em, up or down, one way or the other. These were Martha Stewart's hard core supporters when she embarked upon the long road back from a conviction and prison term to save the brand that she had so carefully and skillfully crafted.

Martha Stewart's missteps are well known and have been documented again and again by the press. Her first mistake was to sell the infamous ImClone stock on a hot tip. Then there was a clumsy cover-up between Martha and her stockbroker who claimed that they had a prearranged agreement to sell if the stock dipped below $60 a share. She followed this episode by violating what some call the first rule of criminal defense: don't talk to the cops.

While she was making these misjudgments in the legal case, she was making equally bad mistakes in the public relations arena which was supposed to be her strength. Susan Magrino Agency, her longtime-public relations firm, seemed overwhelmed by the charges and failed to put out any kind of PR message at all. They claimed the lawyers were calling all the shots. She finally switched to the crisis management firm, Citigate Sard Verbinnen. Within hours of her indictment, Citigate launched marthatalks.com or Martha Talks. Within one year, it had recorded 16 million hits and 81,000 e-mails.

Author Eric Dezenhall, media damage control expert, analyzed Martha Stewart's media problems in an Internet chat, "The Martha Stewart Crisis," on Global PR Blog a few days prior to her sentencing. He felt that a "media feeding frenzy" began after her appearance on CBS' *The Early Show* when she was asked a direct question about the ImClone controversy. This interview was widely regarded among PR professionals as a disaster because Martha acted flip, showed no human depth, and said she preferred to focus on her salad. PR professionals, according to Dezenhall, quickly added this interview to their training tapes on how NOT to answer a direct question.

Dezenhall suggested, "when you live by personality, you can die by personality." He felt that the same doggedness that served her well on the way up, backfired on the way down. He also observed, "you can't tell divas that diva behavior is wrong," when the behavior has been effective at times.

After the CBS infamous salad interview, Martha Stewart went silent. She cancelled public appearances. She broke another rule of crisis management media professionals recognize ,that in a crisis "silence isn't golden, it's guilty." During the lapse into silence, the anti-Martha blogs had a field day with each new detail that emerged about her case.

The anti-Martha blog postings were especially vicious. On a blog called Branding Blog by Dave Young, Martha's stock market knowledge was ridiculed. "The most amazing thing about the Martha Stewart story is that she risked and lost over a BILLION dollars in value of her own company to save about 50 grand in speculation on a medical stock. No wonder she's a former stock broker." He says that fans of fantasy fiction will recall the "Wizard's First Rule . . . People Are Stupid."

In June 2003, Martha launched Martha Talks, the Internet site that was to become her voice during the remainder of the crisis except for two strategically timed interviews with Larry King and Barbara Walters. Up to her sentencing in July 2004, the site had received 34 million hits and 170,000 supportive e-mails. Although she was late getting started, Martha used this form of Internet communication flawlessly. Some media experts thought she should have employed a blog or at least added comments or a bulletin board section to her Internet communication site. But probably the danger posed by allowing the anti-Stewart fans to post on the site was a greater risk. In the end, Martha Talks remained a one-way site except for the receipt of e-mails with only the supportive e-mails being posted.

In retrospect, she may have made a wise decision not to allow posted comments on Martha Talks because the anti-Martha blogs continued to hammer away at her throughout the twenty-three month ordeal. Respondents to Branding Blog chose to attack Martha Talks, her Web site, with comments such as "For Christ sake, someone give Martha a Gag Order." Martha Talks will "inform you of just how guiltless a narcissistic character can be." And another posting stated that "she has no one to blame but herself and her own well developed arrogance. In her case prison is a 'good thing,' she will die a better person and live a better life." The respondent asked for "mercy" on her shareholders.

Martha's strategy was to use her Web page as a spokesperson, and the strategy proved that the Web could be used effectively in crisis communication. She did not have to face her harshest critics directly, she did not have to make many risky personal interviews, and she could tell her side of the story. She was in control of the communication here.

The Web site contained trial updates, statements from Stewart's legal team and collections of opinion and editorials written on her behalf. It evolved into a news source itself without exposing Martha to interviews. As the traffic at the site continued to grow, the number of hits and e-mails the site received were added to the site for immediate attention. The site had a strong effect on mobilizing her supporters, but in the end it failed to sway the jury. She let much of the heavy lifting support be done by her blogging fans like SaveMartha.com. It carried both news items from Martha Talks and posted comments from Martha's most loyal fans, and it kept track of the rise in her company stock prices as the brand image was rebuilt.

Martha Talks succeeded at presenting Martha Stewart as a normal person in sharp contrast to the media honed image of her as the super-heroine of the home. The site was deliberately humble, subtle, and personal. It presented her as a person who realized the serious nature of her legal problems while consistently maintaining her innocence. Even if it failed to sway the jury, it was an island of stability for her and her company

Martha continued to post her messages in Martha Talks after she had been imprisoned in federal prison in Alderson, West Virginia. On December 22, 2004, in a Christmas message, Martha lobbied for criminal sentencing reform and complained about the bad food. But her post contained the same human appeal that characterized Martha Talks. She wrote, "When one is incarcerated with 1,200 other inmates, it is hard to be selfish at Christmas. I beseech you all to think about these women—to encourage the American people to ask for reforms, both in sentencing guidelines, in length of incarceration for nonviolent first-time offenders, and for those involved in drug-taking. They would have been better served in a true rehabilitation center than in prison."

The posting was carefully designed to relate her in-prison experience to her life of the domestic diva. "Cleaning has been my job—washing, scrubbing, sweeping, vacuuming, raking leaves, and much more. But like everyone else here, I would rather be doing all of this in my own home." Also posted was notice that she had asked the U.S. Court of Appeals to overturn her convictions and that the court was unlikely to rule on this before her release from prison.

Eric Dezenhall, the PR crisis management expert, correctly predicted on Global PR Blog that "Stewart will be back." He carefully stated the reasons for his prediction: "Americans enjoy the whole process of crucifixion and resurrection. A wounded Martha may be a lovable Martha. We do love to see the mighty suffer. A Martha comeback would be a story the media would love to do. . . . There are too many examples out there to tell us that scandal is not only temporary, but it could be the best thing that ever happened to someone."

Dezenhall's prediction was right on the mark. Blogs gave Martha high praise for taking her "lumps" and serving her sentence instead of sitting it out while she fought an appeal in court. One said that at the end of the day she did the right thing and that the market would treat her right for it. Another said all the experts who thought Martha's "fifteen minutes of fame" were over after her imprisonment at Alderson had better think again. "Ms. Stewart had proven she has staying power." Her live, hour-long daily TV show; a twenty-four hour radio channel on Sirius; numerous merchandising contracts; and a deal to design and build Martha Stewart homes in planned communities—all these and more prove the point. But not every celebrity has fared so well with blogging support.

PETE ROSE STRIKES OUT

On the PeteRose.com Web site, for $300, a buyer can purchase a Pete Rose autograph baseball with the inscription, "I'm sorry I bet on baseball." To many people, this "collectible" is another of his many attempts to gain fan support for his readmission to baseball and for his long time quest to be eligible for baseball's Hall of Fame. The new autographed baseball looks as if he will try a new strategy of redemption.

After more than ten years of publicly denying that he had ever bet on baseball, the Cincinnati Reds' All Star player and manager publicly admitted on ESPN's *Dan Patrick* radio show that he had bet on baseball both while he was a player and also while he managed the team. He was careful to state that he never bet against his team, the Reds. He "only bet on them to win."

This admission sent a charge through baseball's blogging world. One irate blogger declared, "He's a liar; I don't trust him even when he says he's admitting the truth." Another blogger wondered what he might admit to ten years from now. "At the end of the day, it has yet to be proven that Pete Rose bet on games as a player, and we only have his word, for whatever little it's worth, that he bet on the Reds to win. Ten years ago, he said he never bet on baseball at all. And in ten years, maybe he will admit to having bet on the Reds to lose."

The Hall of Fame organizations honor those who conquer athletics. Eligibility is available to players, coaches, and referees. To be elected, a nominee must be retired and must have made a significant contribution to the game. Eligibility is determined by the Hall, an honoring committee, and a screening committee. Baseball's Hall of Fame takes nominations from the Baseball Writer's Association of America which adheres to similar requirements of eligibility.

In 1920, the Pro Football Hall of Fame, located in Canton, Ohio, began honoring the great players of the professional football world. In 1936, the National Baseball Hall of Fame in Cooperstown, New York, was founded and, in 1939, opened its doors. In 1968, the first Basketball Hall of Fame opened on the campus of Springfield College in Massachusetts. In 1981, a new Hall was dedicated and has inducted fewer than three hundred members to its organization.

Conduct, morals, and ethics are not listed as eligibility requirements for athletes for the Hall of Fame. Today, however, athletes' multimillion dollar contracts hold them responsible to a certain code of conduct so that the team can reap the benefits of the player's contract time and physical abilities. Bonuses can be reduced or forfeited for violations of the code of conduct. The League also monitors players for behavioral habits and fines them according to the violation or offense. Because these great athletes are major role models for youth, a player's behavioral habits get considerable attention from league offices.

Society more than ever seems to have placed off-field activities under scrutiny. Blogs have assumed a major role in monitoring sports behavior just as they have assumed a watchdog role over the media and politics. The public somehow feels it has a right to any information, however unscrupulously obtained, on high dollar athletes simply because of what they earn. Many have no sympathy for the men and women of the games; they have put themselves in the lime light and must deal with the fallout of fame.

Peter Edward Rose Sr., known to the baseball world as "Charlie Hustle," was considered a cinch to be inducted into Major League Baseball's National Hall of Fame. On April 8, 1963, he debuted, and in September 1985, he made his 4,192 hit at home which transformed his career. Rose, a switch hitter, is the all-time major-league leader in hits (4,256), games played (3,562), at bats (14,053), and outs (10,328). His record doesn't end there. He won three batting titles, one Most Valuable Player Award, three World Series rings, two Gold Gloves, the Rookie of the Year Award, and seventeen All-Star appearances. He played five different positions: second base, third base, left field, right field, and first base. As a manager, he won 412 games while losing 373 games.

But even with this amazing record, his career came to a stunning halt. In 1989, after he retired, Rose was banned from baseball for life by Commissioner Bart Giamatti when Rose's bets of thousands of dollars on baseball games both as a player and a manager for the Cincinnati Reds were exposed. An official 225 page report on Rose's gambling charges was released to the media despite the commissioner's assertion that the report was confidential.

On March 19, 2007, in an article on Britannica Blog, Denny McLain, a former thirty-game winning pitcher, asked, "What's So Surprising about Ole Pete Rose?" McLain broke into the league the same time as Rose and remembered running into him at a baseball card show. "Mac," Rose said, "I get up each day and do Pete Rose, and that's enough for anyone."

If anyone did, Rose knew that he was baseball's all-time hit king and he could spend his days signing autographs, talking the game, and simply fulfilling fantasies. Rose admitted to betting on Dan Patrick's ESPN radio show. He said he bet every night, every game. He seemed to repent and sincerely concede to being an ex-ball playing gambler.

On his blog, McLain asked, "What's the big deal, folks? Who ever believed for a moment that he had not bet on baseball? Numerous people had stated this years ago—friends, attorneys, ex-wives, and cops. It seems to me that Pete would be a little relieved that he's finally admitted it."

Pete, a very likeable guy, was the son of LaVerne and Harry Rose who had four children in a working-class community. Harry played semi-professional football and encouraged his son to play sports. Rose played baseball and football in high school, although he struggled academically and had to repeat the ninth grade. His father kept him out of summer school so that he wouldn't miss a season playing ball. He was barred anyway and joined a Dayton amateur club. In 1960, he finally graduated with an impressive record and signed with the Reds.

In 1963, after the season, Rose joined the National Guard and served at Fort Knox. In1964 and again in 1984, he married and had two sons and two daughters. Pete Jr., son from his first marriage, followed in his father's footsteps and spent sixteen years as a minor league baseball player, including an eleven-game run with the Reds.

In 1999, during the trial just before the World Series, Rose received what is said to be the loudest standing ovation ever given to a player. Jim Gray of ESPN interviewed Rose and asked him what everyone wanted to know about the gambling allegations, "When are you going to admit what everyone already knows?"

Jim Gray: Pete, now let me ask you. It seems as though there is an opening: the American public is very forgiving. Are you willing to show contrition, admit that you bet on baseball, and make some sort of apology to that effect?

Pete Rose: Not at all, Jim. I'm not going to admit to something that didn't happen. I know you're getting tired of hearing me say that. But I appreciate the ovation. I appreciate the American fans voting me on the All-Century Team. I'm just a small part of a big deal tonight.

For years Rose continued to deny the allegations. The Commissioner's report stated that in 1985, 1986, and 1987, Rose bet on fifty-two

Cincinnati games at an average of $10,000 per day. In 1985 and 1987, he also concealed income on his tax returns.

In his blog, McLain commented that he had read the report which was very thorough, including photocopies of betting slips, witness accounts, and results of handwriting analysis. McLain also revealed that all League clubhouses posted a sign warning everyone about gambling and the threat of banishment. He even admitted to gambling himself and wrote about off-field events in his book, *I Told You I Wasn't Perfect.*

McLain summarized the tragedy with a final statement, "Pete knew what he was doing—knew what the consequences were and did it anyway. Like the rest of us, he was full of piss and vinegar. But his fatal flaw was that as great as he was, he wasn't bigger than the game itself, and that's something all of us learn eventually. No matter what he tries or says in 2007 or beyond, he will pay the price for his indiscretions forever."

Commenting on the McLain blog, several bloggers agreed. McLain said, "Rose will likely pay for his indiscretions ad infinitum." He observed that Joe Jackson of the old Chicago Black Sox is still waiting for reinstatement and someone sends his name in every year. "Now we have Rule 21 (d), [lifetime banishment for gambling] with signs posted throughout major league ball parks. Pete thought he could beat it. He gambled and lost. He knew the consequences and rolled the dice none-the-less. He lost."

Later, Rose's 322 page autobiography, *My Prison Without Bars,* published by Rodale Press, hit the book stores. In January 2004, Rose admitted to the charges and made a public apology, stating that he bet on Reds games but never bet against the Reds. He appeared on *Good Morning America* and *Primetime Thursday.*" He repeated that statement on ESPN's *The Dan Patrick Show,* saying, "I bet on my team every night. I didn't bet on my team four nights a week. I bet on my team to win every night because I love my team, I believe in my team. I did everything in my power every night to win that game."

In 1978, Billy Joel's song, "Zanzibar," referred to the player in the lyrics: "Rose, he knows he's such a credit to the game / But the Yankees grab the headlines every time." Joel remedied the lyrics in "12 Gardens Live," changing them to "Rose, he knows he'll never make the Hall of Fame."

In his book, Rose stated his version of what happened. On Aug. 24, 1989, Commissioner Bart Giamatti held a press conference at the Hilton Hotel in New York and announced that in accordance with Major League Rule 21, Rose had agreed to be placed on "the permanently ineligible list." Rose believed that the Commissioner would not make any formal findings or determinations on any matters including "the allegation that Peter Edward Rose bet on any Major League Baseball game." The settlement also stated that either side could make public statements "so long as no public statement would contradict the terms of the agreement and resolution."

Shortly after the commissioner announced the settlement, he fielded questions from the media. When asked about his personal opinion, Mr. Giamatti replied that based upon reading the Dowd Report, he believed that Rose had bet on baseball. When he heard that, Rose said, "My lawyers and I were slack-jawed. We felt like we had been slapped in the face." Within hours after signing the agreement, which made "no finding," the commissioner had reneged on his own terms.

Mike O'Sullivan of www.corplawblog.com posted his comments that the settlement agreement prevented Giamatti from making a formal finding or determination. That had nothing to do with his personal feelings. He explained the proof from a legal standpoint.

Contrary to Rose's account, the Agreement and Resolution that Rose signed does contain a finding—an admission by Rose, of all people: Peter Edward Rose acknowledges that the Commissioner has a factual basis to impose the penalty provided herein.

It's difficult to imagine this being anything other than an admission by Rose that he bet on baseball—the only factual matter being penalized. So when Commissioner Giamatti gave his personal opinion that Rose bet on baseball, he was arguably just saying what Rose had already acknowledged in the agreement.

But this is all technical and largely beside the point. Does anyone think the Commissioner of Baseball would go to the trouble of imposing a lifetime ban on a star player like Rose if the Commissioner didn't personally believe the allegations made against Rose? How could Rose have thought anyone would interpret the entire action against him as anything less than a very strong finding that he bet on baseball?

Rose was sentenced to two consecutive five-month prison terms in a Marion, Illinois, federal facility; three months in a half-way house; 1,000 hours community service; a fine of $50,000; and mandated counseling for his addiction to gambling. As for his book, on January 25, 2004, it was a hit at number one on the *New York Times* nonfiction bestseller list.

By remaining aloof and refusing to humanize his plight as Martha Stewart had done or to apologize to his fans, Rose failed to make use of his own or others' blogs for his support. Instead, he let the negative blogs dominate. Blogging contributed to the rejuvenation of Martha Stewart's image and empire; Pete Rose struck out in cyberspace.

"Internet's First Scalp!"

CHAPTER 8

BLOG AS WATCHDOG
Plagiarism, Lying, and the "Internet's First Scalp"

Of all the functions that blogs have performed since they burst on the media scene with the Drudge Report, none has demonstrated its power more directly than this watchdog of society. Blogs have exercised minute scrutiny of politicians, writers, news media, individual reporters, corporations, TV personalities, prosecutors, defendants, and celebrities. The reach of the blogs is tremendous, the response lightning fast, and the effectiveness, if at times unethical, well documented. Blogs get results. One blogger, Rita Desai, has referred to this blogging watchdog phenomenon as "The Age of the Internet: Ruining Reputations in Record Time."

THE CASE OF KAAVYA VISWANATHAN
UNINTENTIONAL PLAGIARISM

Kaavya Viswanathan, a nineteen-year-old student at Harvard University from Hackensack, New Jersey, looked as if she were on her way. A major New York publisher released her first novel, *How Opal Mehta Got Kissed, Got Wild, and Got a Life* (2005). The plot of the novel revolves around a serious, focused Harvard applicant. Opal is an Indian-American young woman told by a Harvard admissions officer that she is not well-rounded. Opal decides to change and become the typical teenager.

In real life, Harvard admitted Viswanathan, and the school newspaper reported that she chose a career in investment banking. Her novel manuscript played a key role in her admission to Harvard. What was still more impressive, her agent parlayed her manuscript into a two-book deal with Little, Brown publishers for a reported $500,000 and a movie deal with Dreamworks.

On April 23, 2006, the wheels came off the track. The *Harvard Crimson* published an article, "Student's Novel Faces Plagiarism Controversy." The newspaper reported that Viswanathan's novel contained "several" passages that "are strikingly similar to two novels written by Megan F. McCafferty." The *Crimson* identified *Sloppy Firsts* (2001) and *Second Helpings* (2003) and offered a specific example from *Sloppy Firsts*: "Yet another example of how every girl had to be one or the other: smart or pretty." They quoted more examples of plagiarism as well in a carefully researched article.

When the Crimson staff reached Viswanathan for comment and confronted her with the accusations, she replied, "No comment. I have no idea what you are talking about." She also failed to return an e-mail request for comment to the paper. The newspaper then contacted the author of the plagiarized material, Megan McCafferty, author of three novels and a former editor at *Cosmopolitan.*

McCafferty responded that she was "already aware of this situation, and so is my publisher." She responded to the newspaper e-mail request: "After reading the book in question and finding passages, characters, and plot points in common, I do hope this can be resolved in a manner that is fair to all parties." Random House, McCafferty's publisher, responded that the publishing house is "taking these allegations very seriously." Viswanathan's novel had just reached thirty-second on the *New York Times* bestseller list when the *Crimson* news story broke.

The next day, Viswanathan admitted to borrowing language from McCafferty's earlier work, but she said it was "unintentional." In a statement released by her publisher, Viswanathan apologized to McCafferty, saying that "any phrasing similarities between her works and mine were unintentional and unconscious." Little, Brown and Company said that future printings of the novel would be revised "to eliminate any inappropriate similarities."

In offering an explanation as to how the plagiarism happened, she seemed to suggest that the plagiarism was some kind of unconscious epiphany:

> When I was in high school, I read and loved two wonderful novels by Megan McCafferty, *Sloppy Firsts and Second Helpings*, which spoke to me in a way that few other books did. Recently, I was very surprised and upset to learn that there are similarities between some passages in my novel and passages in these books.
>
> While the central stories of my book and hers are completely different, I wasn't aware of how much I may have internalized Ms. McCafferty's words. I am a huge fan of her work and can honestly say that any phrasing similarities between her works and mine were completely unintentional and unconscious. My publisher and I plan to revise my novel for future printings to eliminate any inappropriate errors.

Viswanathan's publisher no doubt hoped that this public apology coupled with a pledge to revise future printings of the novel would be sufficient to quiet the controversy over the book. If they did, they were sadly mistaken.

Random House, McCafferty's publisher, found the response from Viswanathan and Little, Brown and Company "deeply troubling and disingenuous." On December 20, 2007, Random House's entire statement was quoted in Wikipedia. The publisher was suspicious of the claim that the similarities were "unconscious and unintentional." They concluded, "The extensive taking from Ms. McCafferty's books is nothing less than an act of literary identity theft." They had no intention of dropping the matter.

Viswanathan's plagiarism was immediately picked up by major news outlets like *Time* and the *New York Times*. Bloggers took to it quickly. Providing a good example of the blogosphere in action, exercising its self-appointed role as watchdog. In only one week, so many blogs worldwide had sprung into action that Tom Zeller, *New York Times* writer, likened it to a "global hive." Zeller explained how the literary bloggers operated with considerable insight:

> In the age of the Internet, literary exegesis (whether driven by scandal or not) is no longer undertaken solely by pale critics or plodding lawyers speaking only to each other, but by a global hive, humming everywhere at once, and linked to the wiki. And if you are big enough to matter (as any writer would hope to be), one misstep, one mistake, can incite a horde of analysts, each with a global publishing medium in the living room, and, it sometimes seems, limitless amounts of time.

In his article, Zeller declared that in the "Internet Age, Writers Face Frontier Justice."

Within a few days of the story breaking, bloggers were pouring over Viswanathan's novel, analyzing it line by line. Within three days, bloggers had added two more authors to the list of books they claimed she had copied from, including Meg Cabot's *The Princess Diaries* and Sophie Kinsella's *Can You Keep a Secret?* The bloggers kept turning up so many plagiarized passages that Wikipedia began keeping a running total and eventually accumulated more than thirty-five passages that they claimed were plagiarized.

But the bloggers did not stop there. With dizzying rapidity, the charges kept on coming until the number of books she was accused of plagiarizing numbered six. The Book Blog at Readers.Read.com reported the climax: "Just when you thought that the number of authors that Kaavya Viswanathan had plagiarized had reached a ridiculous number, we learn of yet another instance of copying. Kaavya also plagiarized the work of Salman Rushdie."

On May 4, 2006, Rushdie told CNN that he thought Viswanathan's lapses as anything but "unintentional and unconscious." He said he could not accept the idea that they could have been accidentally or innocently done. "The passages are too many and the similarities are too extensive. And I am sorry that this young girl, pushed by the needs of a publishing machine and no doubt by her own ambition, should have fallen into this kind of trap so early in her career. I hope she can recover from it."

The sheer weight of all the allegations, accusations, comparative literary analysis, and number of authors involved proved too much for Viswanathan's publisher. When the first allegations came to light and not much was known, Little, Brown and Company stood behind their author. But with the overwhelming weight of the new accusations based on documented plagiarism uncovered by bloggers, media, and authors, the publisher backed down.

Little, Brown and Company recalled all copies of the novel and cancelled Viswanathan's UK publicity tour. The publisher cancelled plans to release a revised printing of her novel with the corrected plagiarized parts. On May 2, 2006, a little more than a week after the plagiarism scandal broke, the publisher announced that it had cancelled Viswanathan's contract for a second book. Dreamworks also cancelled plans for a movie adaptation of the novel.

Because Viswanathan's plagiarism did not involve work that she submitted for academic credit at Harvard, her literary theft did not adversely affect her academic progress at Harvard. The Dean of Harvard College, Benedict H. Gross, told the *Crimson*, "Our policies on plagiarism apply to work submitted to courses, so questions of academic dishonesty would not apply on cases of non-academic work." He also said, "We expect Harvard students to conduct themselves with integrity and honesty at all times."

Even after Little, Brown and Company took the bold step of withdrawing 55,000 copies from the shelves, canceling revisions, and terminating Viswanathan's contract, bloggers and commentators argued furiously about what it all meant. David Edelstein of nymag.com stated that the usual explanations for plagiarism include "accidental copying, occupational or personal stress, or even mental illness." He identified a new one for Viswanathan. Her excuse was being the "victim of a photographic memory." Jennifer Rudolph Walsh, Viswanathan's agent, said, "Somewhere in her mind, she crossed an invisible line with this material and didn't realize that the words so easy and available to her were not her own." Edelstein wasn't buying the excuse. He could see "pinching" one or two phrases in the course of writing a 320-page book; by the time a novelist does it twenty-nine times, the effort is "transparently intentional and conscious."

Some of the bloggers eventually charged racism over the incident because she was a "woman of color." One blog called Selekha.com, "connecting Indians worldwide," summarized some of the opinion that saw Viswanathan as "a victim of ostracism because of her dark skin and Asian background." They compared Viswanathan to the case of James Frey and his book, *A Million Little Pieces*, which remained on the shelves after he was accused of making up and exaggerating many details of his autobiographical story. After he apologized, the story died.

Selekha wondered openly in her blog about possible explanations:

- Is it because Kaavya is of a minority background?

- Is it an apparent failure of the educational system?

- It is the "product of the over-commercialization of writing?"

- Is it a "breakdown of responsible criticism and liberalism in today's society?"

- Is it a "wilt-under-pressure scenario for Kaavya?"

On April 30, 2006, Selekha concluded, "Time to grant her some space and respite from all this mayhem and give her some time to grasp what is going on."

On May 11, 2006, perhaps the last word was submitted by a commentator called "Amused":

Fact of the matter is Kaavya stole a bit from here and there . . . and got caught. God alone knows how many would-be or already plagiarists are out there. Lesson to Kaavya is, write what you can and don't steal. If you get caught, be prepared to take whatever well deserved crap is thrown at you! And remember that all the writers and would-be writers will bay for your blood. Moralists will have a field day and finicky types will analyze your action to death. They won't call a bit of paragraph lifting as a bit of paragraph lifting and be done with it. . . . Such is life!

Kaavya Viswanathan may, by now, know this lesson about plagiarism better than anyone, and she is free to enjoy the substantial educational and monetary profits of her scandal.

JAMES FREY: IS LYING BETTER THAN PLAGIARISM?

Another instance of blogs playing a dynamic role in literary deception and scandal is the case of James Frey, the author of *A Million Little Pieces*. Bloggers discovered the nonfiction book to contain numerous examples of fabrications and falsehoods. Bloggers pounced with a vengeance and beamed a bright light on many of these fabrications until the author admitted that he had exaggerated the facts of his life for literary effect and even admitted that the chief bloggers who exposed his lies had done a good job. He survived the ordeal, unlike Viswanathan, without his publisher having to recall 4.5 million copies from the shelves, suggesting that it may be better to lie than to steal.

In 1969, Frey was born in Cleveland, Ohio, and attended Denison University and the School of the Art Institute of Chicago. On April 15, 2003, Doubleday Books, a division of Random House, published *A Million Little Pieces* by James Frey. This memoir chronicles his life up to, and including, his treatment for drug and alcohol addiction at the famed Hazelden rehabilitation facility. The book received some good reviews, particularly from *The New Yorker* magazine whose reviewer called it a "frenzied, electrifying description of the experience." Amazon.com editors named it their favorite book of 2003.

The big break for Frey and *A Million Little Pieces* came when Oprah Winfrey surprised everyone and chose the selection for her monthly book club. On October 26, 2004, Oprah did a show called "The Man Who Kept Oprah Awake at Night." Oprah declared that everybody at her production company, Harpo Productions, was reading *A Million Little Pieces*, and she aired tear-filled testimonials of how moving the book was.

On the show, Frey told Oprah, "I was a bad guy. If I was gonna write a book that was true, and I was gonna write a book that was honest, I was gonna have to write about myself in very, very negative ways." He did write about himself in negative ways. He announces eight times in the book, "I am an Alcoholic and I am a drug Addict and I am a Criminal," capitalizing these words for effect each time. He claimed he was arrested fourteen times. In a short time, the book had sold 3.5 million copies and was on the *New York Times* nonfiction bestseller list for fifteen weeks, an amazing feat for Frey's first book.

The story turned out to be too good to be true. On January 8, 2006, The Smoking Gun Web site at thesmokingun.com that specializes in publishing the mug shots of celebrities who are caught in various brushes with the law, posted an article entitled, "A Million Little Lies: Exposing James Frey's Fiction Addiction." When The Smoking Gun had tried to find a mug shot of James Frey—which should have been an easy thing to do on a person who claimed fourteen brushes with the law—they were at first unsuccessful. So they started their on investigation into Frey's accounts of his lawlessness.

Little by little, big parts of the book that Frey told Winfrey were "all true" began to be exposed as half true or wholly untrue. Under the intense scrutiny of the investigation, many claims in the book began to appear as outright fabrications. Police reports, court records, and interviews with law enforcement personnel and other sources failed to establish key sections of Frey's books. The Smoking Gun asserted that the evidence they uncovered showed "wholly fabricated or wildly embellished" details of his purported criminal career, especially the suggestion that he had been an outlaw "wanted in three states."

Frey, in his second book, had claimed to have spent eighty-seven days in prison and during that time had polished off *Don Quixote, War and Peace*, and *Brothers Karamazov*, even reading passages of them to a jail mate named Porterhouse. The Smoking Gun investigation could find no record of his ever being incarcerated beyond the five hours it took to process his DWI arrest. He records a melee with Ohio police, but the police who were interviewed thought he was polite and civil. He listed his blood alcohol level at a .36 when records showed he declined to take the blood alcohol test.

Most disturbing of all to the investigators at The Smoking Gun, Frey claimed to have been involved in a tragic railroad accident in which two girls were killed, suggesting that he had been responsible for their obtaining alcohol the night of the accident. Again, police have no record of his involvement, and one police investigator said, "I don't remember Mr. Frey. I don't recognize the name." The Smoking Gun interviewed the mother of one of the accident victims, who said, "As far as I know, he had nothing to do with the accident. I figured he was taking license. . . . He's a writer, you know, they don't tell everything that is factual and true."

Frey made several attempts to limit the damage of The Smoking Gun article. When confronted with the egregious allegations on the day before the investigative report was published online, he refused to address any of the significant conflicts between the uncovered evidence and the claims in his book to accuracy. He confided to Smoking Gun that he had engaged Martin Singer, the Los Angeles attorney, to represent him after an earlier interview with The Smoking Gun staff. The editors at The Smoking Gun responded by publishing the entire five-page letter of the attorney even through they were threatened with "breach of confidence and a violation of the Copyright Act" litigation.

Smoking Gun requested one final interview with Frey prior to publication of their investigation, but Frey refused to grant the interview. Instead, he posted the e-mail on his Web site, bigjimindustries.com, telling his readers of the "latest attempt to discredit" him. "So let the haters hate, let the doubters doubt, I stand behind my book, and my life, and I won't dignify this bullshit with any sort of further response."

Because the Smoking Gun investigators had interviewed Frey twice "off the record" about many of the issues of questionable accuracy, the editors had included a list of these issues in their e-mail to Frey. He published the e-mail and their list of concerns on his Web site in his denial of an interview. For their part, the editors at TSG interpreted his "preemptive strike" as a "waiver of confidentiality" over the interviews that had been off the record. Frey's attempt to limit the damage had backfired.

TSG reported Frey's admission that in early 2003, he had talked to the *Minneapolis Star Tribune*, saying, he "never denied that he altered small details." He claimed that his publisher had fact-checked his work. He also claimed that the "only things I changed were aspects of people that might reveal their identity," though he never told his readers that he had done this.

The Smoking Gun article revealed that Frey declined their request to review court records that Frey claims to possess about his criminal career, saying they had been legally expunged from the record. But Frey admitted the truth of their central charge that he had fabricated details of his criminal career. He admitted to The Smoking Gun that he had embellished details of his criminal career and purported incarceration for "obvious dramatic reasons."

The key allegation in The Smoking Gun report was that Frey had never been arrested except for a misdemeanor drug case. In his account of that arrest, Frey had exaggerated major details of the case. He had not hit a police officer with his car while heavily intoxicated and high on crack; he had not had a profanity-laden melee with numerous officers; and he had not had an eighty-seven-day jail term.

On October 24, 1992, the officer in Glanville, Ohio, who was actually on the scene, filed a police incident report. That gave an entirely different picture of the case. Frey, it reported, had attempted to park his 1989 white Mercury in a no parking zone directly across the street from the Granville firehouse. The right front tire of the vehicle rolled up on the curb.

When Officer Dudgeon approached the car, he noticed Frey was slurring his words. There was a half-full bottle of Pabst Blue Ribbon on the front seat. The officer administered several field sobriety tests which Frey failed. He was then arrested and taken to police headquarters where he declined to take a blood alcohol test. Frey was issued two traffic tickets. One was for driving under the influence, and the other was for driving without a license. He had a separate misdemeanor summons for an open container of alcohol in his car. Frey was released on $733 cash bond which was posted at 4:00 a.m.

The Smoking Gun summarized their findings about the incident that differed markedly from the account in Frey's book:

- There was no patrolman struck with a car.

- There was no urgent call for backup.

- There was no rebuffed request to exit the car.

- There were no swings at cops.

- There was no billy club beat-down.

- There were no thirty witnesses.

- There was no .29 blood alcohol test.

- There was no crack.

- There was no mayhem.

The arresting officer recalled that Frey had even been polite and courteous.

On January 8, 2006, publication of the Frey investigation by The Smoking Gun fueled a firestorm of blog-driven controversy. The aftermath was best described by Writer's Blog with great sarcasm. "I-MADE-it-up memoirist James Frey's new megabucks book deal has exploded into a million little pieces." They revealed that Frey had a two-book deal until it had been scandalously revealed that he had "fabricated much of the story." The deal was cancelled.

On January 31, 2006, Kassie Evashevski of Brillstein-Grey Entertainment announced that she had dropped Frey as his literary manager "over matters of trust." She told *Publisher's Weekly* that she had never "personally seen a media frenzy like this regarding a book before." And the blogs continued to comment.

Finally on February 1, 2006, Random House published Frey's note to the readers, which was to be included in all subsequent editions of the work. In this note, Frey apologized for fabricating portions of the book and for making himself appear "tougher and more daring and more aggressive" than he actually was. He suggested in the apology that he had created this person in his mind as a way of helping him cope. He admitted that he had fabricated for literary reasons. "I wanted the stories in the book to ebb and flow, to have dramatic arcs, to have the tension that all great stories require."

A class action settlement suit was brought against Frey for people who had bought the book under false pretenses. Random House eventually reached a legal settlement by allowing customers who had bought the book to get a refund. On September 24, 2006, MSNBC reported an agreement was reached. On January 20, 2006, the guy who duped Oprah Winfrey had to endure one final appearance on her television show for a "shaming." After that, he was essentially free to enjoy the substantial monetary profits of his scandal—something that even the most conscientious blogs were not able to prevent.

THE CASE OF TRENT LOTT: "THE INTERNET'S FIRST SCALP"

In 2002, no role that bloggers have played as media watchdogs received more national attention than in the ultimate resignation of Trent Lott from his position as Senate Republican leader. Lott became the first majority leader in Senate history to resign under pressure. Bloggers are credited with keeping the story of Lott's offensive, racially-targeted remarks alive when the national media had chosen to let the story slide to the back pages. Blogs provided major historical context for the national debate, and they scrutinized media coverage of the story with a comprehensiveness that was unprecedented. The resulting blogger campaign has been called, admittedly with some exaggeration, "the Internet's First Scalp."

Described in a December 7, *Washington Post* article by Thomas Edsall, the crisis began on December 5, 2002, at the one hundredth birthday party and retirement celebration for Senator Strom Thurmond, Republican of South Carolina, in the Dirksen Senate Office Building in Washington. Thurmond was the oldest and longest-serving member of Congress. Senate Majority Leader Robert Dole spoke first at the event; then came Lott's turn.

In his tribute to Senator Thurmond, Lott made reference to the retiring Senator's failed Presidential bid of 1948 when he had run as a Dixiecrat candidate and carried the state of Mississippi, remarking, "I want to say this about my state. When Strom Thurmond ran for President, we voted for him. We're proud of it. And if the rest of the country had followed our lead, we wouldn't have had all these problems over all these years either." Those gathered at the ceremony applauded when he said, "We're proud," but there was an audible gasp and general silence when he said "we wouldn't have had all these problems over all these years."

No major television network covered Lott's remarks in prime time, but the remarks were carried live on C-SPAN cable network. Indeed, the story might never have been covered at all by any establishment news agency except for a chance occurrence. Ed O'Keefe, an off-air reporter for ABC News, heard Lott's remarks at the party and thought they were news. But he could not get his editors at ABC to do anything more than on December 6 at 4:30 a.m. run a brief news item. The story was caught in the Web of a 24-hour news cycle, plus not having anyone to respond to it, and so it got kicked into the "old news" cycle. O'Keefe's pivotal role in the event is described in "The Legend of Trent Lott and the Weblogs," a blog by Jay Rosen.

O'Keefe's efforts did not go in vain. He succeeded in getting the story online into ABC's "The Note," the most blog-like medium at the network. This achievement proved fortuitous for the whole unfolding story.

Two things happened next to save the story from extinction. A style section reporter for the *Washington Post* covered the party as a society event and informed Thomas Edsall, *Washington Post* writer, about Lott's remarks. At that point, Edsall saw the quote in "The Note," and Rosen reports he began to press his editors at the *Post* to do a news story about the quote for the paper.

Edsall had written *Chain Reaction* (1991), a book about race and American politics, so he was familiar with the reverberation of segregationist voices throughout Southern history, including Strom Thurmond. He was the perfect writer to put Trent Lott's comments in context, to reveal how shocking they actually were.

On December 7, 2002, Edsall wrote the only press article to appear on the subject of Trent Lott's remarks. On page six of the *Washington Post*, Edsall's headline appeared, "Lott Decried For Part of Salute to Thurmond." He reported that Lott had said that in 1948, the United States would have been better off if Thurmond, the "then segregationist" candidate, had won the presidency. Edsall described the setting of Lott's remarks, and then he explored the background of the Dixiecrat political party that Thurmond had represented. Thurmond had declared during the campaign that "all the laws of Washington and all the bayonets of the Army cannot force the Negro into our homes, our schools, our churches." Edsall even found an old party platform that said, "'We stand for the segregation of the races and the racial integrity of each race.'"

Edsall then sought reaction to Lott's remarks from major opinion leaders. William Kristol of the conservative *Weekly Standard* was emphatic. "Oh God," he said, "It's ludicrous. He should remember this is the party of Lincoln." Representative John Lewis, a former civil rights leader, said he was stunned by Lott's remarks. "I could not believe he was saying what he said," referring to Thurmond as one of the best known segregationists. "Is Lott saying the country should have voted to continue segregation, for segregated schools, 'white' and 'colored' restrooms? . . . That is what Strom Thurmond stood for in 1948."

At this moment on December 7, 2002, it appeared that the Trent Lott story would disappear and not be heard from again in spite of the Senator's egregious remarks. Blogger Josh Marshall, who is credited with keeping the story alive, believes that, because of the news cycle of the big media, a news story really has only a twenty-four-hour audition. It has twenty-four hours to catch fire and become a story or become old news and die. Between December 6 and December 10, the Trent Lott remarks became old news to the world of big media, the networks, and the press. According to Marshall, "that story failed its twenty-four-hour audition." He believes that in a "pre-blog world, that would have been the end of it."

Bloggers, according to Jay Rosen of New York University's Journalism Department, entered the picture at precisely the moment that the story was dying in the big media. Josh Marshall, who published his own blog called Talking Points Memo, was among the first of the bloggers to revive and expand the story. He was quickly joined by Atrios and Glenn Reynolds. Collectively, their readership numbered at most 200,000 people.

So these bloggers understood that they were not displacing the big media and the press in what they were doing. In effect, what they did was to take "temporary custody" of a story that had originated in a small corner of the national media and to keep the story alive until it could again garner the attention of the big media. Atrios acknowledged that bloggers had not replaced but actually needed the big media: "For the most part, the influence of blogs is limited to the degree to which they have influence on the rest of the media. Except for the very top hit-getting sites, blogs need to be amplified by media with bigger megaphones."

For three days while the bloggers had temporary custody of the story of Trent Lott, they blogged with a fury. David Frum, the online conservative writer, would call Lott's words "the most emphatic repudiation of desegregation to be heard from a national political figure since George Wallace's first presidential campaign." And the blogging commentary whipped on and on like a firestorm.

Jay Rosen, writer of an online blog at New York University, quotes the political director of ABC news as saying the press in general is not favorable to calling a spade a spade. They would rather have someone else do this and then report it. The press "is usually not in the business of saying, 'Oh my God, this is outrageous.'" It would prefer to have someone else take that step. But journalists will go trolling for strong responses, an act considered within their authority. Blogs are under no constraints of such a system of outsourcing of news judgment. In the Trent Lott story, the blogs immediately expressed their outrage.

The Trent Lott story could not escape the relentless pressure of the blogosphere over a three-day blitz. Josh Marshall uncovered Lott's career of actively supporting segregation during his college career and of making similar statements at various times during his career. Five days after the remarks, the blogger-stoked story reappeared on the national media picked up by major news outlets.

Lott made several attempts to explain his remarks. He at first mildly dismissed it as simply being cordial to the retiring Senator at a party. As criticism worsened, he specifically repudiated his racist past and even claimed his full support for affirmative action. Calls for Lott's resignation began to be heard from both political parties. Some politicians tried in vain to defend Lott, but they were fighting a losing battle.

Finally, even President Bush voiced harsh criticism of Lott's remarks and distanced himself from the Senator, saying, "Any suggestion that the segregated past was acceptable or positive is offensive, and it is wrong. Recent comments by Senator Lott do not reflect the spirit of the country. He has apologized and rightly so. Every day that our nation was segregated was a day our nation was unfaithful to our founding ideals."

Lott later reversed himself and agreed with the President. He apologized for the fourth time. "Segregation," he said, "is a stain on our nation's soul. . . . Segregation and racism are immoral." But the damage had been done and was irreversible. On December 20, 2002, having lost the support of his Senate colleagues and the White House, Lott resigned as Senate Republican Leader barely two weeks from the day he made his Thurmond remarks.

Bloggers had performed a watchdog function as they had never performed in history. Trent Lott was the Internet's First Scalp. Looking back on the event, blogger Josh Marshall, whose blog was instrumental in keeping the story alive, made some observations about why blogs performed well in this instance.

Marshall believes that the conventional news media almost missed the story because of a "journalistic clubbiness." He believes everyone knew all the principal players. "Everybody knew Trent Lott. Everybody had gotten used to Strom Thurmond." They saw Thurmond as a "lovable old guy with a weird accent who had done some bad things way back in his past, but it had all been forgotten." With these blinders on, journalists missed the story.

Blogs were free of these journalistic blinders, Mashall pointed out: "It was up to the blogs, precisely because of their political engagement; also because a blog doesn't need a news peg to return to a story the second day. A newspaper has to have a news peg to come back to a news story the second day. . . . Blogs can keep making the case for a story. They have freedom that conventional news publications don't have. In this case, it allowed them to see a story that needed attention that the big cable networks and the newspapers were blind to."

Bloggers had performed as citizen journalists and watchdogs, taking custody of a news story that the mainstream press was prepared to let slip off its pages. Bloggers revealed that a major story was here and it was right on the surface when probed. They also demonstrated the consequences blogging can generate, negative and positive, sometimes anticipated and sometimes unintended.

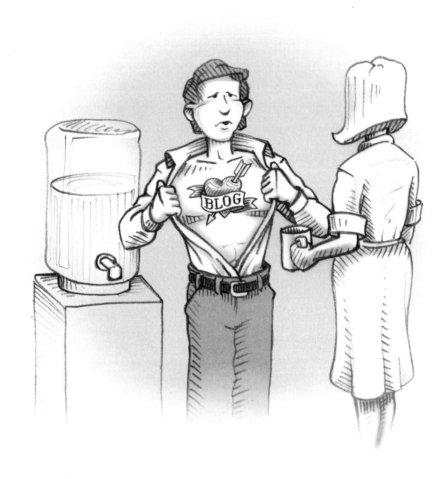

"Sure I regret it now, but at the time . . .
it just felt like the right thing to do."

CHAPTER 9

WHAT *WAS* I THINKING?
THE UNINTENDED CONSEQUENCES OF BLOGGING

> **BLOGGER'S CODE:** BEFORE HITTING "SUBMIT," THINK TWICE ABOUT WHAT YOU ARE
> TRYING TO SAY AND THE POTENTIAL UNINTENDED CONSEQUENCES.

In 1995, Nicholas Negroponte at MIT predicted that the "Daily Me" would soon emerge on the Internet. In this personalized online newspaper, each reader would carefully screen and choose components in advance. Only information that a reader wanted to receive would be included. With just a few clicks, you could have immediate access to sites that show that "you are right to like what you already like and think what you already think."

Through the use of blogs, wikis, and Internet sites, the "Daily Me" is already upon us if not exactly in the form Negroponte predicted. Everyone with a computer, software, and a blog can produce a "Daily Me," personalizing news and views and linking them globally across the blogosphere.

Perhaps no trend of the blogosphere has been more threatening to the traditional guardians of the established media than the personalization that blogs bring to the dissemination of information. In the classical model of news dissemination, there are gatekeepers, like reporters and journalists, who gather the news and tell us what is important. Under this model, a group of people called editors sort through and rank the news. They control everything from the assignment of stories to how they will sound, how they are slanted, and what their prominence may be on the page.

In the world of blogs, the role of editors has been greatly reduced in the news equation. The citizen journalist writes the story which may or may not have a copy editor, and then another person or machine indexes it for easy retrieval. In the world of blogs, the user decides what's important, often determined by the number of hits on the sites and links. This revolutionary shift in the balance of power has not been without consequences for the news and bloggers, and some of the consequences were unintended.

This overwhelming personalization of the blogosphere has taken the form of what author Robert Scoble calls "naked conversations," which he believes are transforming the culture—not always for the better. In *Naked Conversations* (2006), his book about blogging in business, he reports a case of how shocked a blogger was at Waterstone's, a well known British retailer, when the blogger was fired for comparing his boss in his blog to the "pointy-haired manager" in the Dilbert comic strip. The blogger seemed genuinely surprised that such a thing could happen to him for indulging in his supposedly private activity. This case illustrates one of blogging's many unintended consequences, and the cases are growing almost daily.

HEATHER ARMSTRONG GETS "DOOCED"

One of the most celebrated cases of a blogger being fired for something that she had written on a blog is the case of Heather Armstrong who blogged at dooce.com. After she was fired, she coined the term "dooced" to mean a person being fired from a job for something written on a blog. Although she did not identify her company or her coworkers by name, she wrote about her workplace and coworkers frequently, not in flattering terms. She maintained a well-designed sophisticated blog read by hundreds of people.

Biz Stone, author of *Who Let the Blogs Out?*, believes if you end up getting fired for blogging, "you wanted out of that job." In the case of Heather Armstrong, it certainly appears so. Her personal blog heavily mixed blogging and work. One of her postings was called "The Proper Way to Hate a Job" and listed examples of job-hating behavior:

- Wear the same clothes you passed out in the previous night.

- Exercise your right not to shower.

- Arrive an hour late to work, singing, "Smack My Bitch Up."

- Take a two-hour lunch: one hour for the burrito, one for the nap.

And she listed other similar distasteful sentiments in this truly naked conversation.

Perhaps the straw that broke the camel's back was from the same post, stating, "Ignore the inane string of e-mail from the Vice President of Spin to the Vice President of Enabling His Fist Up Your Ass, CC'd to everyone in the company because really what's a cock fight without an audience." A month later, Armstrong made a posting on her Web site titled "Collecting Unemployment." It said, "I lost my job today. My direct boss and the human resources representative pulled me into one of three relatively tiny conference rooms and informed me that the Company no longer had any use for me. Essentially, they explained, they didn't like what I had expressed on my Website."

In Heather's case, it turned out that an "anonymous person" had e-mailed vice presidents in her company to inform them that she had written unsavory things on her "personal Website." She referred to the person who had alerted the bosses of her Web site as a "whistle-blower." Since a blog is a published work available to everyone in the world, she should hardly be surprised at this unintended consequence of her postings.

In her blog postings, she asked her readers' opinions of two issues: should she be accountable to her employer for what she says on her blog when she is careful not to mention specifics and would it be different if the "whistle-blower" turned in a notepad which had the same content? She finally accepted the notion that she had been taking a big risk with her blog and posted the comment: "But I really don't feel like I have the right to be all that bitter. I made my bed; I'll lie in it. . . . I understood the risk when I wrote certain things about certain figures that key members of my company might discover my Website and pooh-pooh my endeavors."

On February 25, 2003, the one-year anniversary of her termination of employment, Armstrong was still blogging away. In honor of the occasion, she asked all of her readers instead of celebrating with vindictive destructive behavior to honor "Happy Dooce Got Fired Day" by selecting one book and one song that they would take with them if they were fleeing a nuclear holocaust. There were 258 posted comments. She posted first with the Van Morrison song, "Tupelo Honey," and the Taro Gomi book, *Everyone Poops*.

As time passed, Armstrong seemed to have developed a deeper sensitivity to the consequences of blogging and of the responsibilities imposed upon her by being one of the country's most read bloggers. In an interview with April Witt, *Washington Post* writer, in the third year of blogging, Armstrong reflected on her early blogging experiences and how she blogged in the beginning. "I talked about having sex. I talked about drinking. I talked about having lesbian fantasies." This was a woman who had grown up Mormon where premarital sex and even caffeine were forbidden.

She said she was sure her family would never find out about her blog because they didn't have Internet access. But her brother got a home computer and discovered her blog. He was stunned. "My mother called me at work. She was bawling for an hour. She couldn't understand what she had done wrong." Her father told her that she was "a vile human being" and "had succumbed to the dark side." He wouldn't talk to her for months.

"I should have learned my lesson then," Armstrong said, but four months later, she was fired for the things she had been writing on her blog about her coworkers and her company. She learned from the experience. Now she says, "I tell people whoever you think is not going to read your Website will find your Website. They specifically will find it and read it and all hell will break loose."

Although she's never stopped chronicling her life, she takes a more sober approach to blogging now. She appears to be much more careful when she posts since she is married and has a new baby. Once she's posted something, it will always exist somewhere in the blogosphere. She says she "still has to remind herself to be her own censor." The blogosphere is a very big place. "The scary thing is that I am on my own computer. I don't see anyone reading it. I don't see their faces."

ELLEN SIMONETTI AND THE NEW TWIST IN EMPLOYMENT LAW

In another highly celebrated case of being fired for posting content on a blog that was displeasing to an employer, Ellen Simonetti, a flight attendant, was suspended from Delta Airlines and then fired for pictures that she posted in her blog, Queen of the Sky.

She told Clubplanet.com that she started the personal blog to help her get over her mother's death. She said she ensured that she made no mention of the airline she worked for and that she created fictional names for cities and companies. The airline's name was changed to Anonymous Airline, and the city where she was based was called Quirksville. She took photographs for the sight with a digital camera inherited from her mother.

When she was suspended by Delta, she removed the approximately ten images from the site. "They did not tell me which pictures they had a problem with. I am just assuming it was the one of me posing on the seats where my skirt rode up." Apparently company policy dictates that the airline uniform cannot be used without prior approval of the company. Ellen Simonetti currently has a case pending against Delta over her firing.

Although Delta Airlines would not comment upon an internal personnel matter, they obviously believed that the postings on Simonetti's blog were inappropriate in some way, and these postings led to consequences. Her case highlights the issue of personal blogging and freedom of expression versus employer rights and responsibilities, an area of the law of the blogosphere that is far from clear. Simonetti took legal action against Delta for wrongful termination, defamation of character, and lost future wages.

These unintended consequences of blogging in the workplace have become so pervasive that they have created a new niche of employment law: handling Internet bloggers who write about their workplace or use blogs while at work. The Committee to Protect Bloggers, an Oregon group who monitor legal actions affecting bloggers, reports that in 2004, eleven bloggers were fired for blog related activities. Companies are noticing that self-published materials, like blogs, can contain confidential company information, that they can defame the corporate image or offend coworkers with easily accessible blogs.

Conservatively, the Pew Internet and American Life Project claimed that in 2004, eight million Americans had blogs and the number has been steadily rising since.

The crux of the conflict revolves around the fact that many employee bloggers believe that blog comments are both anonymous and are also protected within the Internet. They seem to believe that what they are writing is not a whole lot different from what people say around the water cooler. They are ignoring the fact that the audience is comprised of millions.

In a recent court case (*Apple Computer v Does*), a judge ruled that bloggers do not have the same confidentiality protections as journalists. Apple had subpoenaed three bloggers to reveal the identities of anonymous sources who allegedly gave the bloggers confidential information. Just how anonymous bloggers really can be in the blogosphere continues to remain murky, for bloggers and employers.

A SEX BLOG EXPOSED

Nowhere is the case of unintended consequences of blogs more sensational or dramatic than the Capitol Hill case of Jessica Cutler, a twenty-four-year-old mail clerk staffer in the Senate office of Mike DeWine (R-Ohio). Ms. Cutler had studied international relations and once aspired to be a journalist at Syracuse University before coming to Washington and working at several low-level Congressional staff jobs.

On May 5, 2004, Cutler started an anonymous Web log, having a few of her closest friends as the intended audience. She said it would save her from having to e-mail the details of her life to them. She called her blog the "Washingtonienne," and her early entries contained journal postings like this: "I have a glamour job on the Hill. That is, I could care less about gov or politics, but working for a Senator looks good on my resume. And these marble hallways are such great places for meeting boys and showing off my outfits."

The postings on her blog would be scandalously frank and candid. She boasted of having sex with six different men and of taking fees, which she called "gifts," as high as $400. She justified this action by her low salary as a mail clerk. "Most of my living expenses are thankfully subsidized by a few generous older gentlemen. I'm sure I am not the only one who makes money on the side this way: How can anybody live on $25K/year?"

In the gossipy, buzz-filled atmosphere of Washington, D.C., Cutler was able to blog anonymously for barely two weeks before being revealed. On May 18, 2004, her blog was exposed by Ana Marie Cox, the premier gossip blogger of Washington, in her blog, the Wonkette. "Oh my God, you're famous," a friend e-mailed Cutler. "Your blog is on Wonkette." Cox had posted an article on her blog and linked to the Washingtonienne site itself. When Cutler realized she had been identified, she frantically took down the site, but the Internet moves too fast. The blog had already been copied, and it was becoming a blogger's feast, igniting a media feeding frenzy.

In a very short time, the consequences of the exposure of Cutler's blog were felt on Capitol Hill. On May 23, 2004, she was fired for unacceptable use of Senate computers. The *Washington Post* quoted a statement by Senator DeWine that Cutler "had used Senate resources and work time to post unsuitable and offensive material to an Internet Web log."

Richard Leiby of the *Washington Post* was the first to get an interview with the newest sex celebrity on Capitol Hill, and he was anxious to know more about the woman behind all the speculation. Was she really bedding six different men? Who was the married high-level federal employee paying $400 for lunch hour liaisons?

Cutler claimed that what she had written in the blog was true, but that it was really no big deal. "Everything is true," she told the *Post*, "It's so cliché. It's like, 'There's a slutty girl on the Hill?' There's millions of 'em." She declined to provide the name of the man who paid her $400 for sex, saying that she was not trying "to ruin his life." She said it was "more like a gift than it was paying for a service." She expressed amusement and surprise that her blog had taken Congressional staff and Web surfers by a storm for a week. "It's amazing to me that people have any interest in such a low level sex scandal. If I were sleeping with a congressman, maybe, but I'm a nobody and the people I'm writing about are no-bodies."

If Cutler thought the scandal was going to go away with some interviews, she was sadly mistaken. There were more unintended consequences of her blogging diaries.

Cutler had attempted to disguise her sex partners by using only their initials in the blog. Two of her partners were quickly identified on the Internet, as bloggers searched Congressional and federal staff directories. Robert Steinbuch, an attorney who worked for DeWine, and Matt Doyle, a staffer for another Senator, were quickly alleged to be the partners while the search went on for a Chief of Staff with the initial "F." Although Jessica Cutler may have been a nobody in a low-level Washington scandal, she was quickly learning the power of blogs to produce unintended consequences.

The exposure of her blog and the consequences followed a familiar path for sex scandals. There was the familiar six-figure book deal that resulted in the publication of *The Washingtonienne*, her first novel based on her diary blog. There was an offer and a *Playboy* magazine spread, and there were career opportunities in the writing field. Her post-scandal life appeared to be headed up a lucrative path.

Then came another unintended consequence—the possibility of invading someone's privacy on a truly global scale at almost no cost.

Information that formerly traveled across backyard fences and circulated around water coolers and coffee pots now could instantly travel across the globe to millions. Suddenly the defense of anonymity seemed pale against these global numbers.

Almost one year to the day after her blog was exposed by Ana Marie Cox, Jessica Coulter was sued for invasion of privacy by Robert Steinbuch, the former Senate aid who had been identified in her blog by his initials as "R.S." He sued for "public revelation of private facts" arising from the dissemination in the World Wide Web of a "blog."

Steinbuch's suit in the U.S. District Court of the District of Columbia (*Robert Steinbuch v Jessica Cutler*) alleged that Cutler's "public blog" described in graphic detail her ongoing sexual relationships with six men, including the Plaintiff. He claimed he did not know that she was simultaneously engaged in a relationship with another man, "let alone five other men," nor that she was recording the details of her relationship with the Plaintiff on a Weblog, "making those details available to the public."

Steinbuch notes that he was clearly identified by his initials, his religion, his job as Counsel to the Senate Judiciary Committee, his place of residence, and the fact that he has a twin. Discerning readers of Washington blogs had little trouble identifying Steinbuch from the number of details supplied in the blog, making his supposedly private sexual life the subject of newspaper stories, gossip columns, unending blogs, and Internet communication.

Steinbuch's court case highlights one of the central legal issues raised by individuals who believe they have been victimized by blogs. Privacy laws are struggling to catch up with a powerful new technology that makes anyone who is so inclined a global publisher at the click of a mouse. As Andrew J. McClung points out, "Today's technology grants any person—no matter how selfish, irresponsible, or malicious—the power to invade privacy global. . . . All it takes is a computer and Internet access." In "Online Lessons on Unprotected Sex," an article in the *Washington Post*, McClung quotes from the civil complaint of Steinbuch. "It is one thing to be manipulated and used by a lover. It is another thing to be cruelly exposed to the world." McClung believes that in this new modern electronic world there is a new C-word question that lovers need to ask their partners—not condoms, not contraceptives, but "computers?"

Legal experts are watching the outcome of this case to see if it sets any new standards for drawing the line between the right of privacy and the First Amendment right to free speech. They believe that its outcome, if it goes to trial, will have major implications for people who blog as well as for people who chronicle their lives on social networking sites such as MySpace and Facebook—a far-reaching unintended consequence.

WALKING A HIGH WIRE WITHOUT A NET

If there is any remaining doubt that blogging can remain forever an anonymous activity shielded from the public spotlight, the case of Dr. Robert Linderman and his malpractice trail seems to have settled the question: what bloggers write is exactly in the spirit of the Latin term publicare "to make public." The consequences of the act of making something public are not always pretty as Linderman's case well illustrates.

Linderman is a well-respected pediatrician with a prestigious Ivy League degree who also was a popular blogger under the screen name of "Flea," a derogatory name that he said surgeons used to call pediatrician students in medical school. His blogging activities had earned him a reputation to the extent that he would be interviewed and linked to "White Coat Notes," the health care blog of the *Boston Globe* newspaper.

Linderman's life and blog took a dramatic turn when he was sued in a wrongful death case stemming from the failure to diagnose a twelve-year-old patient, Jaymes Binns, with diabetes on March 11, 2002. The patient died six weeks later. The case went to trial on May 9, 2007.

The startlingly unprecedented event of Linderman's case is that he deliberately chose to blog about his experience of going through the trial. Attorney-client privilege notwithstanding, he discussed his experiences, emotions, and opinions about depositions and trial preparation that included advice and communications from his defense team. Legal experts (newyorkpersonalinjuryattorneyblog.com) who avidly read his blogs worried that if the plaintiff's attorneys discovered the blog, he would lose attorney-client privilege over what he had disclosed because it was part of the public record. They also feared he would lose insurance coverage if he lost the case. Attorneys all over the Northeast were blogging about the Flea well before the trial, so the case was well known.

The Flea's posting about the trial contained strong incendiary language that could have an adverse effect on his case. He nicknamed Elizabeth Mulvey, the lawyer for the plaintiff, Larissa Lunt and noticed that she bit her fingernails. In the blog he mused, "Wonder if she's a pillow biter too?" He also described the jury as "dozing off" on occasion.

The Boston Globe.com reported on his case in a story called "Blogger Unmasked." Before the trial began, the Flea wrote about meeting with an expert on juries. This expert advised him on how to act when he was under cross-examination. He was to keep the angle of his chair turned slightly toward the jury. He was to keep his hands folded in his lap, and he was to face the jury when answering questions and answer them slowly. "Answers should be kept to no more than three sentences," they quoted from his blog.

If the case boiled down to his real character, in the Flea's opinion, the plaintiff's case could not prevail. Again the *Boston Globe* quoted his blog before he took it down as saying, "We've said it before and we'll say it again: If the basis of this case is that Flea is an arrogant, uncaring jerk who maliciously neglected a patient, resulting in death, the plaintiff will not win, period. As much of a cocky bastard that Flea may appear in the blogosphere, the readers who have a personal acquaintance with the real 3-D doctor understand how such an approach cannot succeed."

Not everything is known about the conclusion of the Flea's malpractice trial, but a few facts did surface and were reported in the *Boston Globe*. On May 11, 2007, Flea took down all the blog posts from the trial itself without explanation. On the second day of Flea's cross-examination, opposing attorney Mulvey asked Flea whether he had a medical blog.

He replied that he did. She then asked him if he was Flea, and he said he was. On May 16, 2007, drfleablog.com was taken down completely without explanation. It was assumed by the legal community that Mulvey intended to introduce the entire blog in court, including the Flea's unvarnished opinions of lawyers, jurors, and the legal process. The next day the case was settled, presumably with a generous settlement for the plaintiff.

The case of the Flea has had unintended consequences for blogging in the medical community that the Flea himself could not have predicted. The case is a dramatic illustration of how blogging, which is already implicated in destroying friendships, ruining job prospects, and thwarting political careers, could now interfere with serious professional endeavors like medicine.

Dr. Kevin Pho, a Nashua, New Hampshire, internal medicine physician who blogs under his own name, gave his own assessment of the case. As for medical bloggers themselves, he said they are feeling "gun-shy" after Flea's case. On May 31, 2007, he reported in White Coat Notes that he had taken out twenty or thirty posts on his blog just from reading what happened to Flea. But he said since he blogged under his own name, he always had to be more tempered in his own blog. "I think it is a mistake to assume that people won't find out who you are. You can assume there's no anonymity on the Web. People can find out who you are." He also said he didn't blog about patients. "I don't want any posts to come back and bite me."

The case has also had unintended consequences in the legal profession as well. Some lawyers who followed the case now warn their clients that their blogs can come back to haunt them whether they think they are anonymous or not. This case was one where law and medicine collided. As Kevin Pho said, "It's a little bit sad in a way. The whole purpose of blogging is to be open and pull back the curtain to talk about how it really is. So the question is, how realistic is that? I think that's what physicians and other health professionals are wrestling with right now. It's a part of the growing pains of the medical blogosphere."

BLOGGING IN THE UNIVERSITY

Since universities are known to house free thinkers, it is not surprising that blogs would make their impact felt in the halls of academe and that the blogging would lead inevitably to unintended consequences. One case which fits this description involves Erik Ringmar, a senior lecturer at the London School of Economics. His case can be pieced together from an article in the *Beaver*, the student newspaper, on May 2, 2006, and an article by Donald MacLeod in the *Guardian Unlimited* on May 3, 2006.

On March 22, the controversy began when Ringmar was invited to address a London School of Economics Open Day event for prospective students. He made controversial remarks about the school and then posted the entire lecture on his blog called "Forget the Footnotes."

The *Guardian* reported that he made a "passionate plea" for a great institution, and he even said, "If you come here, you will be a part of this extraordinary multicultural collection of bright and fun and ambitious people." This seems harmless enough for a recruitment speech, but what followed greatly upset his university officials.

To the prospective students, he said, "I know that we are expected to sell our program to you. An undergraduate is today worth £3000 and there is competition between universities for this money. Unfortunately I don't have a sales pitch. In fact, I don't have a PowerPoint presentation."

He then went on to warn the students about certain realities of a "great institution such as ours," saying the truth is always "the best recruiting tool." He spoke openly of the realities of what the requirement to publish does to the teaching of undergraduate courses. He says, "First class teachers usually have their minds elsewhere than on undergraduate teaching." They might be away at conferences, and if they are not "absent in body, they are absent in mind." He even said that students might have more interaction with faculty at an institution like the London Metropolitan University. But he said the reason to choose the London School of Economics was the first class students.

Needless to say, Ringmar's recruitment lecture posted on his blog went over poorly with his bosses at the London School of Economics.

It excited the wrath of his immediate superiors. On March 24, he was reprimanded by George Philip, Convener of the Government Department in an e-mail. Philip said Ringmar's speech raised the question of whether he really wanted these potential students to come to the school. He also said, "You embarrassed your colleagues," and the e-mail contained an informal oral warning to "destroy/cancel your blog entirely and shut the whole thing down."

Ringmar at first appears to have taken down or edited some of the offending material, but as he continued to gain support from bloggers and students on campus like Facebook users, he put it back up in some form and decided to make a stand on the issue of freedom of speech. On March 27, he contacted Howard Davies, the head of the school, by e-mail, expressing his belief "that a great school such as ours benefits from critical scrutiny," and that he was "keen" to make sure that what he did was in "accordance with School rules."

Davies replied to the e-mail, saying he believed that the blog was damaging to the School and found the blog to "contain criticisms of your colleagues." Davies framed the issue this way. It was not about blogging or not blogging; it was about whether "a colleague can publicly abuse his employer and colleagues without consequences." Once again the public nature of the blog was a crucial issue. In only two months from the time the controversy started, the blog had been visited 10,000 times by 2,620 visitors, most of them expressing overwhelming support for Ringmar.

He won an uneasy truce in the matter. The ban on his blog was lifted, and he continued to campaign for a "Bloggers Charter." He started a new blog which, while far-reaching in content, appears more restrained and less controversial. Apparently both the institution and the blogger learned valuable lessons from this experience about responsible use of blogs.

THE TRAGEDY OF MEGAN MEIER

Blogging has demonstrated power to disrupt the workplace, create a host of new professional concerns, and bring new legal and ethical issues to the forefront of society. Indeed, it can wreak havoc with widespread unintended consequences on friends, families, coworkers, employers, and unsuspecting individuals. But in its most elemental form, it has proven it has proven the power to destroy life.

Such was the case of Megan Meier who committed suicide on October 16, 2006. Megan was a thirteen-year-old St. Charles, Missouri, teenager who posted and received messages on her MySpace page. Through postings, she established a friendship with "Josh Evans," the online name of a fictional character created by Lori Drew, the mother of one of Megan's friends, to discover surreptitiously what Megan might be saying about Lori's daughter.

According to ABCNews.com the fictitious relationship soon turned hostile. Megan got messages saying that she was a "slut" and that she was "fat." Finally on October 15, 2007, the day before her suicide, she received a message from "Josh," saying, "I don't know if I want to be friends with you any longer because I hear you're not nice to your friends." The next day Tina Meier discovered Megan's body hanging in a closet, and she died the next day.

After the unintended tragic consequence of this cruel cyber hoax, the parents of Megan Meier have been campaigning for measures to protect children online. "There needs to be some sort of regulations out there to protect children. Parents can be in only so many places and so many times."

The Megan Meier case reveals the tragic consequences of a deliberate cyber hoax specifically designed for malevolent purposes. However, Web sites and social networking sites can also function as blogs in disguise, feeding and editing information flow for controlled purposes—not always noble. Entries in the Wikipedia Web site, for example, have been notoriously commandeered by opponents of political candidates, editing content to support the opposition's positions. When this happens, Wikipedia operates like an unregulated blog, merely posting comments of the last user who visited the site for editorial purposes. When such a condition exists, the facts are frequently not corroborated, the spin is not stated in an even-handed voice, and the agenda of trying to besmirch a reputation is only a click away.

153

When I was in high school and was preparing a book report, I went to the one and only true source for facts—the *Encyclopedia Britannica*, a real book—not an online collection of words on a screen. This definitive encyclopedia solicited articles from major authorities in fields of knowledge, screened those articles with an editorial board who exercised quality control over content, and used an editorial staff extensively to fact check all entries. Today, our online parents and students alike go to what they think is a spin-off of the *Encyclopedia* called "Wikipedia—the Online Encyclopedia." The online editable aspect of Wikipedia puts quality control in the keyboard of the last person to edit the text. That person may be a responsible person, a lazy person, or a person motivated by malicious intent.

My own Wikipedia entry site is riddled with falsehoods because the freedom to edit makes it little more than a blog. Out of the last fifty edits made to my Wikipedia site, all are from folks that are adverse to my political efforts. In fact, over 98 percent of these comments are being made by three people who are actively working for candidates that opposed me when I tried to get my name on the ballot for Congress last year. I make no attempt to update my entry because software alerts the opposition when any change has been made, and all they have to do is go back and cut and paste previous material. It becomes a game to some to see how quickly they can change back the Wikipedia page to the prior, venom-filled comments. Life is simply too short to spend all of my time focused on correcting the errors and intentional mistakes, unless I have a campaign full of thousands of staff whose job is to update and make such corrections in an active campaign.

For blogs to be truly responsible, they must be transparent as to author and motive. Sitting alone before a computer pouring thoughts, reactions, and fantasies into a blog may seem like a solitary activity, but the millions of potential readers around the world can turn a personal exercise of free speech into communication with severe unintended consequences.

| PART IV |

CALL TO ACTION IN CYBERSPACE

"Don't even think about posting that, mister!"

| CHAPTER 10 |

BEHAVING AS YOUR MOTHER TAUGHT YOU
A BLOGGER'S CODE OF CONDUCT

BLOGGER'S CODE: ACKNOWLEDGE THAT MODERATING THE COMMENTS POSTED ON YOUR BLOG IS A MATTER OF PERSONAL RESPONSIBILITY, NOT AN INFRINGEMENT OF SPEECH.

"Is it too late to bring civility to the Web?" Brad Stone posed this question in his article in the *New York Times* titled "A Call for Manners in the World of Nasty Blogs" (April 9, 2007). The article reflected a movement by some high profile bloggers to establish a Code of Conduct for Bloggers—to try to bring some civility to the nasty, sometimes barbaric, world of the blogosphere.

What prompted the movement by people like Tim O'Reilly, a Web specialist, to call for a code of responsible use was a blogging incident that got out of hand in Boulder County, Colorado. Kathy Sierra, a high-technology author from Boulder, received death threats on blogs, causing her to cancel some public appearances. The matter was turned over to authorities. The *Times* reported that death threats stemmed from a dispute over whether deleting impolitic and inflammatory comments left by visitors on someone's Web site was acceptable or constituted censorship.

The dispute escalated to the point of a blogger leaving manipulated photographs of Sierra next to a noose on some Web sites. She even said she was considering giving up blogging altogether. In an interview with the *Times*, she said she could not just dismiss the incident with the argument that "cyberbullying" is so common on the Web that she should just completely ignore it. "I can't believe how many people are saying to me, 'Get a life, this is the Internet.'" Without pursuing it, she wondered how a blogger can distinguish real threats.

The blogosphere now constitutes one of the most dramatic, successful communication forms in history. The *Times* reports that Technoratic, a blog-indexing company, estimates that at present there are 70 million blogs that add more than 1.4 million entries per day. This number represents staggering growth from the fifty or so blogs in existence when the Drudge Report first fired off the shots that created blogging as a major personal publishing force.

Menacing media communication behavior like that experienced by Kathy Sierra is not exclusively an Internet product. All we have to do is look at political talk radio for behavior that sometimes goes over the top. Shock radio hosts seem to encourage abusive callers. But online conversations seem to be more prone to degenerate into ugliness than those in other media because the Web offers the option of anonymity with no accountability. According to the *Times*, the same factors that make unfiltered conversations so compelling in the first place—and impossible to replicate in the off-line world—"allow them to spin out of control."

THE ELEMENTS OF A BLOGGER'S CODE OF CONDUCT

Blogging is a highly creative outlet for those who do it, and those who master the art are rewarded by local, national, and even international visits and posts to their sites. Unfettered conversational speech provides an air of personalization rarely found in conventional media reporting. Inherent in these strengths of blogging, however, are some elements that give rise to its major weaknesses.

ANONYMITY

Among the most difficult problems facing the blogosphere at the moment is the delicate problem of anonymity. The fact that many comments are posted anonymously is a problem that lurks at the center of many of the blogosphere's controversies. Bloggers have been fired from their jobs for blogging anonymously about their workplace when the blog was discovered, personal blogs with private information on them have had harmful consequences, and all manner of malevolence has been shielded under the cloak of anonymity.

The anonymity of a blogger makes nearly impossible evaluating the objectivity of posts, establishing the credibility of the witness to an event, or determining with any certainty when information is clearly prejudicial. The veil of secrecy provides too great a temptation for a medium that has precious few checks and balances.

The anonymity of the individual who posts comments on a site constitutes an even greater problem. Although some of these posts identify the author, a great many leave comments anonymously, compounding the problem of secrecy. Adding to this problem is a large number of anonymous posts left by "trolls," someone who posts controversial messages in an online community with the intention of baiting others into an emotional response. Some "trolls" will even have multiple aliases and post numerous comments as if several people are chiming in on a conversation. However, the conversation is all one person, merely speaking to himself. Trolls have been a long-standing problem for the online community.

Blogs do not subscribe to the checks and balances of ethics and quality control that other media face. No mandated ethical or quality oversight or controls exist. Bloggers face little restriction, monitoring, or editing of what they write. Legal problems surface only after the harm has been done to reputation, accuracy, and credibility. Anonymity frequently shields bad behavior and malevolent intentions.

RESPONSIBILITY

In the blogosphere, many accept that individuals take responsibility for the words they post on their own blogs, no matter how much or how little quality control, fact checking, or editing went into the post. In fact an acronym, YOYOW, circulates in the blogosphere for "You Own Your Own Words." Debatable, however, is how seriously some bloggers practice this axiom, but for many it is a working principle.

The most complicated issue of blogging and personal responsibility involves the position a blogger takes about what gets posted on his blog by others. Some bloggers do not believe that their personal responsibility extends to the length of deleting inflammatory comments. To these bloggers, deleting any comments at all for any reason would amount to censorship.

Others believe that not only do they own their own words on their blogs but that they also own every post made on the blog by others. This ownership extends to the tone that they allow on any blog or forum they control. To them, this responsibility is part of owning the effects of their behavior and the editorial voice they try to foster. In discussing his proposed "Blogger's Code of Conduct," Tim O'Reilly has found that frequently in a blog that tolerates mean comments there is a "quick race to the bottom." Comprehensive responsibility for the entire conduct of the blog—blogger postings and all comments—is a crucial element in establishing a more civil code of conduct for the entire blogosphere.

The reluctance to delete inflammatory comments from postings means some bloggers have avoided responsibility by using legal protections. Bloggers are protected by Section 230 of Title 47 in the *United States Code* from litigation for posted comments on their blog. Ironically, this section was a part of the Communication Decency Act of 1996.

DELETING UNACCEPTABLE CONTENT

Perhaps the most controversial element in attempting to develop a code of conduct and responsibility for the blogosphere remains the question of deleting unacceptable content from a blog without raising the specter of censorship and the inhibition of free speech. Almost from the beginning, a libertarian ethos has dominated blogging and the unencumbered free-spirit approach to the task has made many bloggers reluctant to interfere with blogging's extreme excesses even when they acknowledge their destructiveness and harm.

Other bloggers have deleted comments and stated clearly that they do not accept unmoderated comments. The *Times* reported that Heather Armstrong, who has been blogging since 2001, stopped posting unacceptable comments on her blog in 2005 because she found that conversations among visitors consistently deteriorated into vitriol. She also had to deal with an anonymous blogger who began a parody of her site and even copying pictures of her daughter.

One of the central questions of the blogger's code of conduct is this: Would the blogosphere and society at large be better served if all bloggers took full responsibility for everything that appeared on the site including links? Would society at large be better served if every blogger's site contained this statement: "We take responsibility for our own words and reserve the right to restrict comments on our blog that do not conform to our standards" (blogging.wikia.com "Responsibility for our own words")? Such a standard would place a heavy responsibility on blog owners for their words and what happens on their sites. It would constitute a major change for large numbers of unmoderated blogs.

CONTENT THAT ABUSES, HARASSES, STALKS, OR THREATENS OTHERS

An obvious standard to include in a code of responsible conduct would be that any posting or comment on the Internet that would abuse, harass, stalk, or threaten another person would not be allowed by the community of users. Although many commentators do not endorse abusive practices on the Internet, they fear censorship more. They worry about who would be the person or entity that determines what is abuse or a threat. They point with great pride to the fact that the Supreme Court struck down the Communication Decency Act of 1996 with the argument that "governmental regulation of the content of speech is more likely to interfere with the free exchange of ideas than to encourage it."

The proponents of a code of responsible conduct point out that they are not advocating governmental regulation of the Internet, just a voluntary code of civility which itself might encourage even more free speech on the Internet. The question for proponents of a code like Tim O'Reilly is how to "encourage both personal expression and constructive conversation." His critics at tnl.net.blog charge him with trying to "clamp down on disagreement through that dangerous weapon called civility." In the blogosphere there are still those willing to tolerate abuse, harassment, threats, and stalking in the name of free speech.

CONTENT THAT IS LIBELOUS OR KNOWINGLY FALSE

According to the "Legal Guide for Bloggers" published by the Electronic Frontier Foundation, defamation is "a false and unprivileged statement of fact that is harmful to someone's reputation, and published 'with fault,' meaning as a result of negligence or malice." Libel is written defamation, and slander is spoken defamation. An opinion cannot be defamatory, but merely labeling something as an opinion does not necessarily make it so. A court would consider whether a listener could construe the statement as asserting a statement of verifiable fact.

The blogosphere is an environment loaded with examples of excess in reporting on public figures, and in defamation law there is a difference between private and public figures claiming defamation. A private figure, such as your neighbor or your roommate, has to prove that you acted negligently. In other words a reasonable person would not have published the comment. Public figures must show a higher standard of injury. They must show that an individual acted with "actual malice" or in reckless disregard for truth according to the "Legal Guide for Bloggers."

Proponents of a blogger's code of conduct would like to see bloggers exercise more responsibility in reducing the amount of the libelous and knowingly false information that is placed on blogs about public and private figures.

CONTENT THAT INFRINGES UPON ANY COPYRIGHT, TRADEMARK, OR TRADE SECRET

Any code of conduct and responsibility, almost everyone agrees, must protect the intellectual property of copyrighted works, trademarks, patents, or trade secrets just as they are currently protected in published works. The current Copyright Act also has maintained a long established provision for allowing "fair use" of a copyrighted work provided it meets certain tests. The Copyright Act states that "fair use . . . for purposes such as criticism, comment, news reporting, teaching (including multiple copies for classroom use), scholarship, or research is not an infringement of copyright." Bloggers make frequent use of the fair use provision of copyright and often link to works that are copied completely. Proponents of a Code of Conduct decry this practice as clearly illegal.

There are no hard and fast rules for determining fair use, but there are some guidelines that refer to percentages of a work and set number of words that are sometimes used. The Copyright Act sets out four standards for a court to use in making a determination:

- The purpose and character of the use,
- The nature of the copyrighted work—factual in nature or fiction,
- The amount or substantiality of the portion used, and
- The effect on the market or potential market.

This fourth standard is often considered the most important. As in the cases of plagiarism, the appropriation of another's ideas is a major form of theft taken seriously, and aggressively pursued, by publishers.

VIOLATION OF OTHERS' PRIVACY

One of the most contentious issues in formulating a code of responsible conduct for bloggers is what constitutes invasion of privacy by disclosure to the public. A person's sexual orientation, a sex-change operation, or a private romantic encounter could all be private facts. Once they are publicly revealed by the individual experiencing them, however, they move into the public domain.

According to the "Legal Guide for Bloggers," a private fact is newsworthy if some reasonable members of the community could entertain a legitimate interest in it, and courts have found that the public has a legitimate interest in almost all recent events. Bloggers have used a wide net to gather private facts.

This wide interpretation of private facts becomes more complicated when bloggers are also journalists. Blogging software can be used for journalism, but not all bloggers take advantage of it this way. The distinguishing characteristic is that "what makes a journalist a journalist is whether she is gathering news for dissemination to the public." Some states have laws that specifically protect the speech and privacy rights of journalists such as reporter's shield laws and fee waivers for the Freedom of Information Act requests.

Bloggers can fall under the standard that courts have used to determine whether someone who invokes the reporter's privilege has that right. Federal courts have used the test of whether the person intended to disseminate information to the public and whether the intent was present at the beginning of the newsgathering process. One thing is absolutely clear in this process: blogging has greatly blurred the line between the journalist and the citizen journalist, and the right of privacy for citizens has been harmed in the process. A code of responsible conduct for bloggers should address this concern.

There are, then, many factors to consider in determining a blogger's conduct standards. Should a blogger's code consider the complete elimination of anonymity—for both postings by the blogger and comments from readers? Should a blogger's responsibility extend to deleting inflammatory comments and other unacceptable content that appears on his or her blogs, or should all be moderated by the owner? Should toleration of abuse or threats be permitted in the name of free speech?

GUIDELINES FOR RESPONSIBLE AND ETHICAL BLOGGING

Since there are many different kinds of bloggers, sampling some of the thinking from specialist bloggers like those in companies can illustrate how everyone is struggling with this issue. At Microsoft, a company that in March 2005 had 1,500 employees who blogged, one of these employees, Robert Scoble, wrote a book called *Naked Conversations*. He includes what he calls his "Corporate Weblog Manifesto" which contains his principles of corporate blogging.

Many of his thirty-four principles are relevant for a blogger's general code of conduct:

- Post fast on both good news and bad.

- Have a thick skin.

- Use a human voice—not corporate PR professionals and lawyers to modify your speech.

- If you screw up, acknowledge it fast.

- If your life is in turmoil and/or you're unhappy, don't write.

- If you don't have the answers, say so.

- If you have information that might get you in a lawsuit, consult a lawyer before posting, but do it fast.

- Be nice to everyone.

- Be transparent. Show you have nothing to hide.

- Disclose all conflicts and biases.

- Keep confidences. If someone says this is not for your blog before telling you something, don't write about it.

- Be clear when you're speaking for your company.

- Be ethical.

- Realize that you don't have free speech if you are identified as a member of a corporation.

- It is always risky to attack the boss.

- Have a conversation with your manager before you start and find out what type of blogging he will defend.

All kinds of bloggers would be well advised to apply these suggestions whether or not in the corporate world.

To help bring civility, legality, and fairness to the blogosphere, I propose a set of "Guidelines for Responsible and Ethical Blogging," voluntary behaviors which I hope will be adopted to curb the harmful excesses mentioned in this book. Many of the suggestions in these guidelines come from the good work done previously by Tim O'Reilly in his "Blogger's Code of Conduct" and Robert Scoble's "Corporate Weblog Manifesto" along with Web discussions of the major issues they raise.

MY GUIDELINES FOR ONE NATION UNDER BLOG

- Operate your blog as transparently as possible, requiring valid e-mail addresses for comments.

- Take full responsibility for all aspects of your blog, including everything that you post and the comments you allow on your blog.

- Acknowledge that moderating the comments posted on your blog is a matter of personal responsibility, not an infringement of free speech.

- Define unacceptable content as anything used to abuse, harass, stalk, or threaten.

- Eliminate content that is libelous, defamatory or knowingly false or that misrepresents another person.

- Follow all fair use guidelines and laws in respect to copyright, trademark, trade secrets, or patents of any third party.

- Honor all obligations of confidentiality both individual and corporate.

- Respect the privacy, publicity, morality, or any other right of a third party.

- Ignore the trolls whose aim is the deliberate inducement of an emotional response.

- Don't say anything online that you wouldn't say in person.

- Before hitting "submit," think twice about what you are trying to say and the potential unintended consequences.

- Do not use a blog willfully to cause harm.

- Be ethical.

- Be careful with legal issues.

- Tell the truth, the whole truth, and nothing but the truth.

Applying these guidelines to the blogosphere, though admittedly an enormous task, I believe, will prevent some major problems with blogs and bring a sense of decorum to an environment that at times has characteristics of the Wild West.

BLOGGING, THE FUTURE, AND OUR CHILDREN'S SAFETY

In his movie, *Kindergarten Cop*, actor and later Governor of California, Arnold Schwarzenegger teaches his young students to yell "Stranger! Stranger!" when they sense any kind of danger. The Internet, with all its enticements, makes identifying those strangers almost impossible, and our children are at risk as a result. As we look to the twenty-first century and all the innovations in communications that we cannot even envision now, the safety and education of our children should dominate our concerns.

Perhaps the most serious abuse issue comes from child predators stalking children on Internet communities like Facebook, MySpace, and other social networking sites that our children enjoy to connect with their friends—and often strangers in disguise. *Dateline* broadcast a vivid example of the enormity of this problem by filming a sting operation in California. In a short forty-eight-hour period, law enforcement officials arrested fifty-one offenders that actually came to what they thought was the home of a thirteen-year-old child. The only initial source that they had to make contact was a single chat room.

The Internet has given the world huge benefits, and we want our children to take advantage of all of them, to be prepared for their lives in a world of swiftly evolving communication technology. While our educational institutions and technology suppliers are training our children to thrive personally, professionally, and internationally through the use of technology, we must also prepare them for the "strangers" they may encounter in cyberspace. Whether these dangers exist in the form of sexual predators, fraudulent information, enticements into destructive behaviors and activities, or ridicule and bullying by word and image, parents have the responsibility to protect their children by teaching them the signals that should prompt them to shout "Stranger!" both literally and figuratively.

Even one small piece of personal information like their school name, their team jersey number, or their e-mail address may mean too much information being available to the public. Our responsibility as adults and community leaders is to make sure our young adults understand the potential dangers. We must help them realize that what seems like innocent chatting with friends can breed negative consequences. Just as we learned that hitting "send" too quickly can distribute e-mails to readers never intended and that e-mails can linger long after we have pressed "delete," so we must be the mentors of our children in their use of blogs and all the other wonders of the Internet.

We can teach them that the "*New York Times* headlines test" works best. If what you are writing is something that would not look good as a headline for the world to see, then don't write it. We must help them resist Web sites that provide a "home page" environment for teens to post their photos and to fill in blanks with answers to questions that automatically populate a personal Web site available to anyone. In an effort to be humorous or simply as a result of peer pressure, young people sometimes even answer provocative questions, without any notion of the consequences of their actions. Often these answers, photos, and comments come back to haunt them when friends, teachers, college recruiters, and prospective employers discover the sites. In short, "free speech" in cyberspace is not always "free."

Blogging holds a special place in the "stranger" world because of the anonymity, creativity, conversational and intimate tone, and the lack of control or regulation. Before we can teach our children responsible use of the Internet, we must be certain we are behaving as model bloggers, following principles of accountability and recognizing the far reaching consequences of what we write. To be effective parents, we must first be responsible adults.

As *One Nation Under Blog* suggests, the powerful technology of blogging can be used for purposes good and bad, useful and ineffective, and hopeful and sinister. But we should not lose sight of the fact as David Kline in *Blog!* has pointed out that the "citizen-expert," "the citizen journalist," and the "informed amateur" in many realms of knowledge and human endeavor gain prominence as a result of the blogging phenomenon. At the same time, "crazies and irresponsible people are also gaining access to wide audiences as are people with evil and criminal intent." There is also an overabundance of "trivial drivel" in blogs. In spite of all of this, the ordinary citizen on a national and global basis is engaging in the lost art of the public conversation. *One Nation Under Blog* is offered in the spirit of making that public conversation better.

Free speech remains at the heart of democracy, and blogging rapidly is becoming the "people's voice." The challenge has always been balancing individual expression with protecting the rights of others. As with any new development in any arena of our lives—medicine, transportation, entertainment, or communication—we are constantly faced with the question: Has our capacity for innovation outpaced our capability of using it wisely? Just as citizenship gives us the right and duty to vote, free speech gives us the right and duty to be responsible.

Sources and Further Reading

ı   *Adams Family Papers: An Electronic Archive.* Massachusetts Historical Society

ı   Brookhiser, Richard. *Alexander Hamilton*, American. New York: Simon & Schuster, 2000.

ı   Brown, Ralph A. *The Presidency of John Adams.* Lawrence, Kansas: University Press of Kansas, 1975.

ı   Caro, Robert. *Master of the Senate,* New York: Alfred A. Knopf, 2002.

ı   Dallek, Robert. *An Unfinished Life: John F. Kennedy, 1917–1963.* New York: Little Brown, 2003.

ı   Dallek, Robert. *Lyndon B. Johnson: Portrait of a President.* New York: Oxford University Press, 2004.

ı   Donald, David Herbert. *We are the Lincoln Men: Abraham Lincoln and His Friends.* New York: Simon & Schuster, 2003.

ı   Ferling, John. "Cliffhanger: The Election of 1800," *Smithsonian Magazine.* November 2004   http://www.smithsonianmagazine.com/issues/2004/november/cliffhanger.

ı   Flexner, James Thomas. *Washington and the New Nation 1783-1793.* Boston: Little, Brown and Company, 1970.

ı   Ford, Paul Leicester. *The True George Washington.* Philadelphia: JB Lippincott, 1898.

ı   Goodwin, Doris Kearns. *No Ordinary Time, Franklin and Eleanor Roosevelt: The Home Front in World War II.* New York, Simon & Schuster, 1994.

ı   Goodwin, Doris Kearns. *Team of Rivals: The Political Genius of Abraham Lincoln.* New York: Simon & Schuster, 2005.

ı   Joesten, Joachim. *The Dark Side of Lyndon Baines Johnson.* London: Peter Dawnay, 1968.

ı   Kline, David, and Daniel Burstein. *Blog: How the Newest Media Revolution is Changing Politics, Business and Culture.* New York: CDS Books, 2005.

ı   McCullough, David . *Truman.* New York: Simon & Schuster, 1992.

ı   McDonald, Forrest. *The Presidency of George Washington.* Lawrence, Kansas: University Press of Kansas, 1974.

ı   McLain, Denny. *I Told You I Wasn't Perfect.* Chicago: Triumph Books, 2007.

ı   Nevins, Allan. *The Emergence of Lincoln,* 2 vols. New York: Scribner, 1950.

ı   O'Donnell, Kenneth P. and Powers, David F. *Johnny, We Hardly Knew Ye.*

Boston: Little Brown, 1970.

| Peterson, Merrill. *Thomas Jefferson and the New Nation: A Biography*. New York: Oxford University Press, 1986.

| Pew Internet & American Life Project, 2004.

| Richers, Maggie. "Honor Above All." *National Endowment for the Humanities*, 2005. http://www.neh.bov/news/humanities/2007-5/honor.htm.

| Rhodehamel, John. *The American Revolution: Writings from the War of Independence*. New York: The Library of America, 2001.

| Rose, Pete. *My Prison without Bars*. New York: Rodale Books, 2004.

| Scanlan, Laura. "Alexander Hamilton: The Man Who Modernized Money." *National Endowment for the Humanities*.

| Schwartz, Barry. George Washington: *The Making of an American Symbol*. New York: Free Press, 1987.

| Scoble, Robert, and Shel Israel. *Naked Conversations: How Blogs are Changing the Way Businesses Talk with Customers*. Wiley: Hoboken, N.H., 2006.

| Stone, Biz. *Who Let the Blogs Out? A Hyperconnected Peek at the World of Weblogs*. New York: Simon & Schuster, 2004.

| Tindall, George and Shi, David. America: *A Narrative History*. New York: W. W. Norton, 2006.

| Wood, Gordon S. *Revolutionary Characters: What made the Founders Different*. New York: Penguin Books, 2006.

| Woods, Randall. LBJ: *Architect of American Ambition*. New York: Free Press, 2006.

| Woods, Randall, and Gatewood, Willard. *America Interpreted: A Concise History with Readings*. New York: Harcourt Brace College Publishers, 1998.

ACKNOWLEDGMENTS

This book would not have been possible if not for a number of folks who helped shape it along the way.

As a proponent of public-private partnerships, I felt that this book endeavor should be no different. I always acknowledge the federal, state, and local contributors to any successful project, and as an author, I wish to do the same.

One Nation Under Blog addresses personal freedom as well as public safety. Freedom to express an opinion and the right to be safe from predators and protected from libel or slander are on a collision course in cyberspace. Where does one begin and the other end? To minimize the carnage generated by the unintended consequences of this collision, concerned citizens at all levels—public, private, non-profit, federal, state, local—are combining their efforts to protect our liberties and our families.

NATIONAL SUPPORT

On a national level, I thank the office of the Attorney General for support as we rolled out an Internet Safety Program to roughly 1,300 cities across America. We merely performed the role of public servant to make sure that the voice was heard to help protect our youth. The numerous staff members within the Department of Justice who worked closely with us were always there to help, no matter the time of day, and no matter how difficult the request.

As we launched the Internet Safety Program nationally, many of the materials were created in conjunction with, and reviewed by, the National Center for Missing and Exploited Children. Ernie Allen, President and CEO should be given an award for all of the children that his agency has saved and protected. Thank you for your willingness to share the wonderful NetSmartz information.

Cities which supported this project faced a challenge because their fiduciary responsibility limits the use of city assets or revenues for the benefit of those beyond their geographic boundaries. As a result, when we desired to roll this Internet Safety Program across America, we knew that we needed the financial assistance of a nationwide company that had the desire and interest in keeping people of all ages safe on the Internet. When I approached Comcast, Brian Roberts, Comcast's Chairman and CEO, responded in less than twenty-four hours with a statement of support "at all cost." If not for the hundreds of thousands of dollars of cash and in-kind support from Comcast, we would not have touched as many folks as we have. Because of your efforts, Comcast, children are sleeping safe tonight.

Serving as mayor afforded me the opportunity to participate in wonderful organizations and meet remarkable people. To the U.S. Conference of Mayors and its entire staff who have provided much guidance and assistance to me and our city, I am most grateful. As a result of the working relationship with roughly 1,300 cities across America, we were able to use their infrastructure to connect with and roll out a nationwide Internet Public Safety Program. Tom Cochran, the U.S. Conference of Mayors' CEO; Trenton Mayor Doug Palmer; Miami Mayor Manny Diaz; and Seattle Mayor Greg Nichols—thank you for your leadership of this fine organization.

Finally, to the CEO of Waste Management, David Steiner, and the Chairman of America's Promise Alliance, Alma Powell, thank you. Both Waste Management and America's Promise Alliance have acknowledged the Sugar Land Internet Safety Program and the Mayors Youth Advisory Council for its coveted Livability Award. Sugar Land's listing as one of America's Top 100 Best Communities for Young People reflects support like yours.

STATEWIDE SUPPORT

On a statewide basis, I acknowledge two friends for whom I have a great deal of respect and admiration: Texas Governor Rick Perry and Texas Attorney General Greg Abbott. Governor Perry and I have had numerous conversations about strategies we needed to implement throughout Texas in an effort to protect our youth, both on and off the Internet. Joining in these efforts is Texas Attorney General Greg Abbott who has made his mission targeting child predators on the Internet and has developed a team of Cyber-crime Detectives that is equivalent to a well choreographed dance ensemble as they seek to apprehend and prosecute these criminals. General Abbott, I have enjoyed working with you and your entire staff on these very worthwhile efforts.

LOCAL SUPPORT

Locally, I acknowledge a handful of bloggers in the Texas Congressional District 22. You have raised my awareness that there is no need to let the facts get in the way of telling a juicy story. *One Nation Under Blog* grew out of what I learned from you: if the facts don't support the story you're trying to tell, then simply make things up! If not for these folks, I don't think I ever would have truly understood the impact—both positive and negative—of the use of blogs in political campaigns, in business, and in life in general. To these bloggers, I say thank you.

A few years back I approached our City Manager, Allen Bogard, with a proposition of how we could benefit our community by creating a Mayor's Youth Advisory Council. The city's benefit could come from the knowledge and advice we could gain from these youth, but of equal importance, Sugar Land could benefit from these youth becoming an asset and advocates for our community. When this idea was brought before our city council, they quickly concurred that the benefit of this program would far outweigh the costs. Allen and my fellow council members, thanks for your wisdom, guidance, and belief in this dream. Our community is much better today as a result of these youth, as they have worked to create an award-winning Internet Safety Program that I am confident has protected people and has saved lives across America. To the members of the Mayor's Youth Advisory Council, far too many members to list here, in the words you taught me: "You Guys Rock!"

If you want your community to be one of the safest cities in the nation, you have to "talk the talk, and walk the walk" in law enforcement. Sugar

Land Chief Steve Griffith, as the chief of police for the fifth safest city in America, you should be proud of your contributions to Internet Safety. In a time when you had plenty of challenges within your department, you could have very easily said that you had higher priorities. Yet when you agreed to perform the "Internet sting operations," your priorities were correct as you issued countless arrest warrants, and arrested numerous people who came to our city with ill intent—via the Internet. Chief Griffith, just think of the lives that you have touched.

The city of Sugar Land has over six-hundred of the finest employees. The quality of life that a citizen comes to expect in a city is not only because of the leadership of the city council. The quality of a community is realized because of the care and pride of ownership of each and every city employee in every department. For each of these fine individuals and friends, I say thank you. The one city employee with whom I spend an enormous amount of time, and who is my liaison to the Mayor's Youth Advisory Council, is Judy Kimrey. Judy, years after I am no longer serving as Mayor, I will think about you daily and wonder how many people you have impacted in such a positive way.

Amy Goldstein, when we first sat down to discuss this book, we thought about how history would have been changed forever if the Internet was around at the times of our "founding fathers." I loved the cerebral discussions that we had doing the "what if" game. You did so much of the research and provided some wonderful thoughts and ideas. I am amazed at how quickly you were able to gather so many factoids, and I always looked forward to your information so I could have another history lesson. The speed at which you could provide this information illustrates the positive side of the Internet.

Writing a book has taken many hours away from my life and my job. I am very fortunate to have a business partner who has been understanding when I am on the computer doing research about the Internet or on the phone discussing writing strategies with the publisher. Costa Bajjali, thank you for being such a great business partner and being so understanding about the time commitment. The best is yet to come, my friend!

This book would not have been possible without the expertise of my publisher, Milli Brown, at Brown Books Publishing Group. Her entire staff continue to amaze me with their insight, creativity, and diligence. Thanks to all, whose contributions in various and numerous ways made my publishing experience a special one.

Last, but of course not least, I would like to thank two other people who have forever impacted my life through hard work, a positive outlook, and many spiritual prayers. My Chief of Staff, Rosemary Mascarenhas, deserves thanks for all of her talents, wisdom, and advice. I have known Rosemary and her entire family for over fifteen years, and we have all been through some pretty great, and some less than great, times together. I am forever grateful and blessed with your friendship and support. Rounding out the rest of the "Dream Team" is Sharon Ehrenkranz. Sharon, I have never seen anyone with as much energy and desire to help out a community as you. Rosemary, you wind me up and tell me where to go. Sharon, you put the words in my mouth. Together, we can climb any mountain.

To all of my great friends who care deeply about our community, I thank each of you for making a large, and very important, contribution to our society.

God bless all of you.

ABOUT THE AUTHOR

David Wallace served three terms as the Mayor of Sugar Land, Texas, completing his tenure in July 2008. Wallace was also appointed by Department of Homeland Security Secretary Chertoff to the U.S. Department of Homeland Security Advisory Council. Additionally, he served as co-chairman of the U.S. Conference of Mayors' Homeland Security Task Force.

Appointed by Texas Governor Rick Perry, Wallace serves on the Board of Directors and as Vice President of the Texas Economic Development Corporation. Wallace is the Chief Executive Officer for Wallace Bajjali Development Partners, LP.

Wallace's involvement in Sugar Land's nationally recognized Internet Safety program led him to focus on the issue of freedom of speech and how it affects our personal freedoms of safety and decency. Wallace's concern for this issue, along with the birth of the blog and its unintended consequences, was the impetus for him to write *One Nation Under Blog*.

Wallace has lived in Sugar Land, Texas, since 1993 with his wife, Kathy, and two daughters.